FROM CHAOS TO CONTROL

DR. OZGUR ERTEM

Publisher Cosmo Publishing
UNITED STATES OF AMERICA

August 2025

Contents

Abstract

This is not your typical project management book.

It's a deeply personal, sometimes heartbreaking, and often humorous journey through the life of Dr. Ozgur Ertem, a tech leader who used project management principles not just to build systems, but to rebuild himself.

Blending storytelling with strategy, this book explores how tools like stakeholder maps, risk registers, retrospectives, and roadmaps can be used far beyond the boardroom to face grief, handle burnout, and depression, plan weddings, ace exams, survive career pivots, and even let go of failed side hustles.

Packed with practical takeaways, interactive tools, and deep human reflections, From Chaos to Control will help you lead the most important project you'll ever manage: your own life.

CHAPTER 01

Introduction: Welcome to the Project of Life

"Life is a journey of evolving projects. The road is long, winding, full of risks and milestones, but it's yours to manage."
—Dr. *Ozgur Ertem*

1.1. Life is the Ultimate Project

Let's be honest, most of us don't wake up thinking,
"Today, I'll manage my life like a project with a work breakdown structure, risk log, and stakeholder matrix."

But in reality, we already do.

Without realizing it, we've been project managers of our entire lives.

Think about it. Have you ever planned a trip, a wedding, a relocation, or even just survived a chaotic Sunday brunch with picky guests, clashing schedules, and an oven that ignored cooking times like it was on strike? Congratulations. That's project management in its rawest form: uncertainty, multiple stakeholders, time pressure, limited resources, and a strong likelihood of something going hilariously wrong.

In fact, I'd argue that **life is the most complex project you'll ever manage**. There's no fixed scope. The objectives keep changing. The stakeholders (family, friends, bosses, kids, in-laws, random LinkedIn connections) are constantly moving the goalposts. The risks are high, the communication plans are fragile, and the timeline? Let's just say it's not always under your control.

Still, we try to deliver.

Every. Single. Day.

Now, I know what you're thinking. "Project management? That sounds like something my company forces me to do with awkward templates, soul-sucking meetings, and Gantt charts that no one ever updates." And yes, I've seen that version of it too. But here's the thing: **real project management isn't about bureaucracy. It's about clarity, momentum, and getting sh*t done.**

It's about defining what matters, setting priorities, planning around chaos, adjusting when life throws curveballs, and keeping your sanity intact.

Let me take you back for a moment.

I didn't grow up with stability. I lost my mom to heart failure when I was young, and my dad to cirrhosis a few years later. Life didn't come with a manual or a backup plan. What I had was grit, curiosity, and a deep desire to make things work somehow. Looking back now, I realize I was already applying the core of project management: figuring out what I wanted, identifying the obstacles, creating a rough plan, and moving forward step by step.

I didn't call them "milestones" or "resource plans." I said things like, "If I study hard, maybe I'll get into that school," or "If I save three more months, I can afford that toy."

But the mindset? It was the same as we now call project thinking.

Fast forward to today, I've worn many hats: engineer, manager, mentor, speaker, author, and above all, learner. I've led multi-million-dollar programs with international teams, organized my own cross-country moves, rebuilt my mental health after burnout, and yes, even started a failed side business that taught me more than some of my actual degrees.

What connects all these? Project management.

And I don't mean the textbook kind. Not the dry theory buried in certifications. I mean humankind, the kind that gets you through Monday mornings, keeps a relationship intact during deadline season, and helps you rebuild your confidence after life knocks you down.

That's what this book is about.

It's not a guide for project managers. It's a guide for humans.

Because if you're reading this, you're already managing projects, you just don't call them that.

Maybe you're navigating parenthood (hello, multitasking). Maybe you're leading a team, launching a startup, buying your first home, or simply trying to figure out what to do next in life. Whatever it is, **project management tools can help you not only survive it but thrive in it**.

And the best part? You don't have to change who you are to do it. You don't need a certificate. You don't need a fancy title. You just need a willingness to see your life through a different lens, one that brings clarity, confidence, and progress.

So, in this book, I'm going to take you through my life in chronological order, and I'll share moments that were joyful, stressful, inspiring, painful, and hilariously messy. Each chapter will focus on a different phase of my life, a different "project," and show how a specific project management principle helped me through it.

From negotiating with my parents as a kid to changing careers. From planning my wedding to surviving a pandemic. From publishing my first book to recovering from burnout, every story has a method behind it. And don't worry, it's not going to be boring.

There will be no endless jargon, no painful diagrams (okay, maybe just one fun visual or two), and no preaching. Instead, you'll get real stories, relatable lessons, a few facepalm moments, and practical tools you can apply to your own life, whether you're a full-time professional, a student, a parent, a dreamer, or a beautiful combination of all of the above.

And by the end, my hope is simple:

That you'll stop feeling overwhelmed by everything you have to do.

That you'll stop questioning whether you're "good enough" to chase the things that matter to you.

That you'll start treating your goals, your time, and your energy with the same respect you give to corporate projects or job tasks.

Because guess what?

Your life is the most important project you'll ever manage.

And it deserves to be led with clarity, courage, and purpose.

Let's begin.

1.2. What This Book is About

Life is a project; messy, emotional, unpredictable, and sometimes planned. Let me tell you exactly what this book is... and just as importantly, what it isn't.

This isn't a traditional project management manual.

This isn't a guide full of charts, equations, and frameworks you'll forget two pages after reading them.

This isn't a corporate textbook designed to impress consultants.

This book is about **you**.

It's about how **the everyday chaos of life can be approached with the calm clarity of a project manager.**

It's about **navigating decisions, setbacks, relationships, careers, and personal growth using tools and mindsets that actually work.** And it's about doing that in a way that feels human, imperfect, humorous, and real.

From the Boardroom to the Bedroom Closet

If you've ever stared at your calendar, trying to fit a dentist appointment between a critical deadline and your kid's school recital, you've done resource planning.

If you've ever compared prices for three different air fryers for three straight nights only to return to the first one, you've performed a cost-benefit analysis.

If you've ever said, "Let's just sleep on it," you've instinctively applied risk mitigation to your relationship.

The truth is, we're all using project management principles all the time, we just don't realize it. This book will show you how to use them on purpose, with less stress and way more control.

Stories, Not Slides

This isn't a book about memorizing tools. It's about remembering stories.

I'll be sharing **personal, sometimes painfully honest, sometimes hilarious, and always real stories** from different stages of my life. These are moments where I either triumphed or tripped over my own shoelaces, but in every case, I came out the other side wiser because of the project management mindset.

You'll read about:

- How I applied stakeholder management to convince my parents to buy me a new toy.
- How I navigated career confusion, eventually leaving engineering behind for project leadership.
- How I managed a wedding (hint: the chaos was very real).
- How I survived a move to another country, and then another one.
- How I used PM principles to get through burnout, depression, and rediscover my purpose.
- How a failed business attempt taught me more than a dozen successful ones.
- How I wrote my first book, powered with sticky notes, sprints, and stubbornly blocked calendar sessions.

I'm not sharing these stories because I think my life is special. I'm sharing them because they reflect what many of us go through, just with different vocabulary.

My hope is that you'll see **your own story in mine**, and more importantly, that you'll start seeing your challenges, decisions, and goals through a more empowered lens.

One Chapter, One Technique

Each chapter is structured like a mini-project.

You'll get:

- A **real-life story**, sometimes funny, sometimes vulnerable, always useful.
- A specific **project management principle or tool** that helped in that situation.
- A section called **"Key Takeaways"** to help you remember the core lessons.
- A **"Try This in Your Life"** practical exercise to take the idea and make it yours.
- In some chapters, you'll even get **visuals or tools** to sketch out your own version of the solution.

I want this book to be something you can **come back to over and over again**, not just read once and put on the shelf. Think of it like your personal life-project companion. A field manual for the real world. The type of book you scribble notes in, fold the corners of, or quote from when someone asks, "How are you managing all this so well?"

Not Just for Project Managers (But Also for Project Managers)

You don't have to be in a project management role to benefit from this book.

You could be a student, a stay-at-home parent, a retiree, an entrepreneur, a freelancer, or someone who's just trying to figure things out day by day.

That said, **if you are a project manager**, you'll likely see your tools in a brand-new light. This book might just help you reconnect with **why you fell in love with structured thinking in the first place** and how to apply it beyond Jira tickets and stakeholder updates.

This is a Book About Hope (Disguised as Planning)

Project management, at its core, is about **believing that things can be better if you plan intentionally, act with focus, and adjust when needed**. It's about creating outcomes instead of waiting for life to happen.

It's about saying, "This is the direction I want to go, and I'm going to build the best path I can with what I've got."

That mindset has saved me, not once, but many times.
It helped me get through exams when the odds were against me.
It helped me rebuild when my health was on the line.
It helped me pivot my career, support my partner, buy a home in a foreign country, and keep dreaming even when things didn't work out.

If it helped me, I truly believe it can help you too.

So, what is this book really about?

It's about learning to **lead yourself** the same way you'd lead a great project. With purpose. With adaptability. And most of all, with heart.

Let's start building.

1.3. Why You Should Care: The "Aha!" Moment

You might be nodding along or thinking,
"Okay, Ozgur. Life's messy, structure helps. But do I really need project management? Isn't that just a work thing?"

Let me be brutally honest here: **if you've ever been overwhelmed, stuck, stressed, stretched thin, or asked yourself "what do I do next?" this book is 100% for you**.

You don't need to be in tech, finance, consulting, or construction to benefit from project management.

In fact, **most of the people who need project thinking the most are outside of those industries**, because no one ever teaches them these tools. We're expected to plan our lives, navigate relationships, raise families, make career decisions, manage health, and chase dreams... but somehow, we're not taught how to plan, prioritize, and execute without losing our minds.

That's where the "aha!" moment comes in.

It's the moment when you realize:
"Wait a minute, I've been project managing my life all along. I just didn't realize I could be doing it better."

You Already Do This Every Day, You Just Don't Call It That

Let's run a quick self-check. Think about the last few days.

- Did you make a to-do list and cross off tasks? ✅ That's a task tracker.
- Did you set a deadline for yourself, like finishing something before the weekend? ✅ That's timeboxing.
- Did you juggle conflicting priorities, like work meetings, laundry, and a sick pet? ✅ That's resource management.
- Did you talk to your partner, boss, or friend to align expectations? ✅ That's stakeholder communication.
- Did something go wrong, and you found a workaround? ✅ That's issue resolution.

See? You're not just surviving. You're managing.

But what if you could do all of that **with more intention, less stress, and better results**?

The Hidden Cost of "Winging It"

Look, I've done it too.

There were times when I thought I didn't need to plan.
I could just go with the flow. Be spontaneous. Figure things out as they come.

And sometimes that works, until it doesn't.

Until you forget something important.
Or overcommit.
Or let anxiety spiral because there's no clarity.
Or you feel stuck, staring at your phone while time passes and opportunities fade.

That's the hidden cost of winging it: cluttered mind, scattered focus, slow burnout.

Once I realized that the techniques I was using to lead complex programs at work could also be used to manage my own energy, goals, relationships, and self-care... it changed everything.

Structured Thinking Creates Emotional Freedom

Here's the twist no one expects:
When you bring structure to your life, you don't feel restricted, you feel free.

Why?

Because planning reduces anxiety.
Because clarity creates confidence.
Because structure lets you **breathe**, knowing you've thought things through.

It's like having a map on a road trip. Sure, you can take detours. But when you know the general direction, you feel less lost, and more in control.

Project management does that for your life.
It doesn't erase the chaos; it gives you a compass to move through it with grace.

Everyone Has a Project That Matters Deeply

Maybe for you, it's:

- Finally making that career move you've been thinking about for years.
- Writing your first book or launching your own thing.
- Getting your health back on track.
- Learning to say no more often and yes to yourself.
- Building stronger relationships.
- Moving abroad. Changing fields. Starting over.
- Or just figuring out what truly matters and how to build a life around it.

Whatever it is... you can **build it better**.

You don't have to hustle blindly. You don't have to wait for permission. You don't need perfect conditions.

You just need a mindset, a way to approach your life like a project worth investing in.

Your Aha! Moment Might Be Right Now

If you've made it this far and something inside you is nodding along, thinking, *"Yeah... maybe this could actually help me..."* then you've already had your first shift.

That quiet inner voice saying, *"Maybe I could take more ownership. Maybe there's a better way."*

That's the moment I live for as a mentor, a coach, a friend, and a human being, because that moment changes everything.

From there, **it's not about being perfect, it's about getting better on purpose**.

So yes, this book is about project management.
But more than that, **it's about your power to choose how you show up in your own life**.

To stop drifting.
To start deciding.
To build, shape, and lead, not just survive.

That's why you should care.

And that's why I'm inviting you to keep turning these pages.

Because the most important project you'll ever lead... is **you**.

1.4. How This Book is Structured: The Roadmap

You're still with me, and that means this idea is clicking with you.

Now that you've had your first "aha!" moment, let's talk about **how this book is laid out**, because just like in any well-run project, clarity on the process makes all the difference.

Think of this book as a **project manual for managing life**, one story at a time.

But not the stiff, 300-page corporate kind with indecipherable jargon and bullet points that make your eyes glaze over. This is **a human, emotional, practical guide**, written like we're sitting across from each other at a cozy café, sipping coffee, laughing about our missteps, and figuring out how to make life a little more manageable, and a lot more meaningful.

Let me walk you through what to expect.

📖 Each Chapter = A Real-Life Project

Each chapter is anchored in a true story from my life, sometimes hilarious, sometimes heavy, always real.
And in every story, I'll show you how a specific project management principle helped me through it, either at the time or in hindsight.

We'll go chronologically through different phases of life, from my early days negotiating toys with my parents, all the way to career pivots, failed side hustles, international moves, marriage, burnout recovery, and building a future vision rooted in purpose.

Some chapters will have laughter.
Some will sting a little.
But every one of them will leave you with **something useful** to take away.

What's Inside Each Chapter? The Structure Behind the Stories

To make the journey even more actionable, I've designed each chapter like a mini life-skill project you can learn from.

Here's the breakdown:

1. A Personal Story

I'll start by telling you what actually happened, and there will be no sugarcoating. Real life. Real stakes. Real consequences.

2. The PM Principle That Made the Difference

I'll break down the specific **project management concept** that helped me handle (or mishandle) the situation. This could be things like risk assessment, stakeholder mapping, scope control, time blocking, agile iteration, or setting up a project roadmap.

Don't worry, **I'll keep it jargon-free and practical**, even if you've never opened a project plan in your life.

3. Key Takeaways

A crisp, no-fluff summary of what you can learn from the experience, even if you've never been in that exact situation.

4. Practical Exercise – Try This in Your Life

Here's where things get powerful.

Each chapter will include a hands-on activity, a reflection prompt, or a small challenge to help you **apply what you've just read to your own life**. You can use these as journal entries, conversation starters, or decision-making tools. Think of them as mini project plans for your real-life scenarios.

5. Bonus Tools & Visuals (in some chapters)

Where it makes sense, I'll include **visuals, simple tools, or creative diagrams** to bring ideas to life. I'll also give you **extra resources and reading materials** if you want to dive deeper.

This way, the book becomes more than a good read; it becomes **a toolkit** you can come back to whenever life feels like a little too much.

🎯 No Prerequisites. No Titles. No Gatekeeping.

Let me say this loud and clear:

You do **not** need to be a certified project manager.
You do **not** need a background in business or tech.
You do **not** need to memorize terminology or follow a specific methodology.

This book is for **real people dealing with real life**.

If you've got challenges to tackle, goals to achieve, or just a bunch of overwhelming stuff to sort through, you're in the right place.

📖 Read It Straight Through or Jump Around? Your Choice.

Some readers will want to follow the whole journey, chapter by chapter. Others might prefer to skip straight to the parts that speak to their current situation, whether it's navigating burnout, switching careers, or managing a big life change.

Both approaches are totally fine.

This book is written to be flexible.
Read it like a story.
Use it like a guide.
Keep it close like a friendly mentor whispering, *"You've got this."*

🛠 The Tools You'll Walk Away With

By the end of the book, you'll have:

- A fresh perspective on how to structure your chaos.
- Real-life examples of PM principles in action.
- A better understanding of your own patterns.
- A more confident, intentional approach to personal and professional decisions.
- A custom-made toolkit for leading the most important project you'll ever manage is **you.**

And just like in any great project, **progress matters more than perfection**.

This book isn't here to tell you to get your life 100% figured out.

It's here to help you **move forward with clarity, purpose, and a little less panic.**

Final Thought Before We Move On:

You now know how the journey is laid out. You've seen the roadmap.
The stories, the structure, the tools, they're all here waiting for you.

But just like in life, nothing happens until you start.
And you're already here, reading this.

So, let's dive in.
The first project kicks off in the next chapter, with a kid, a toy, and a surprisingly strategic negotiation plan.
(Yes, there were stakeholders. And yes, I'll tell you how it went.)

CHAPTER 02

The First Project Plan: Convincing My Parents for a New Toy

"You can learn many things from children. How much patience you have, for instance."

—Franklin P. Jones

My first real project didn't involve a budget meeting or an executive sponsor, just a desperate kid, a dream toy, and two skeptical parents.

2.1. The Toy I Absolutely Had to Have

I still remember it vividly.

The lighting in the store, the exact position on the shelf, the way it called to me like destiny wrapped in plastic and promise. For some kids, it was a train set. For others, a remote-controlled plane. For me, it was the **LEGO of an Off-Road Car 4x4**, an absolute beast of a build, with shock absorbers, chunky tires, and a tiny winch in the front that, in my eyes, made it basically a real vehicle.

It wasn't just a toy. It was *the* toy.

This wasn't the type of LEGO set you finished in 30 minutes and then forgot under your bed. No, this was a serious build. **A multi-hour operation requiring focus, planning, dexterity, and patience.** (Yes, I used that exact line later when trying to sell the idea to my parents.)

But there was a problem.
Actually, two.

Problem #1: My parents.
Problem #2: The price tag.

I didn't grow up in a household where "I want it" was a winning argument. My parents were always kind but pragmatic. Money had to be spent wisely. Toys were a luxury. If I wanted something this grand, I'd need a full-blown business case.

I had two choices:

1. Sulk.
2. Strategize.

I chose the second.

What I didn't know at the time was that this would become my **first unofficial project plan**, a delicate dance of emotional intelligence, stakeholder persuasion, and pitch-perfect timing.

And so began my first attempt at managing a full life project, with passion, patience, and some creative truth-stretching.

The Campaign Begins

I didn't just launch into it with "Can I have this?"
No, this required tact.

First, I tested the water with my dad. I told him about how **I'd been doing really well in school lately**, how I'd **helped set the table without being**

asked, and how I was **really getting into engineering for the future** (which may have been a stretch). I mentioned casually how **this particular LEGO set helps develop reasoning and cognitive agility**, a line I'd heard from a commercial and clung to like a lifeline.

"It's not just a toy," I said. "It's like... training for a future career in robotics. And engineering. Maybe even architecture?"

That, of course, was pure fiction.
I just wanted to build it, admire it, maybe race it across the floor, and feel like I owned something awesome.

But hey, **fabricated feature-benefit mapping is a classic** sales move. Even adults do it every day on PowerPoint slides.

Timing Was Everything

I learned early on that timing was just as important as the pitch itself.

For instance, presenting this request right after a heated discussion about the electricity bill? Not ideal.
Trying to lobby for a toy while my mom was preparing dinner? Also, a terrible idea.

But Sunday mornings... now those were golden.

There was something about the slow pace of a weekend morning, the smell of black tea in the air, and everyone being just relaxed enough to consider an outrageous idea.

That's when I launched the second wave of my campaign, this time with my mom.

But not both of them at once. I had learned that parents, when united, were an impenetrable wall. I needed to soften them up **individually** before attempting the final stakeholder alignment meeting.

Objection Handling (a.k.a. Crisis Management)

The objections were inevitable and arrived like clockwork:

- "It's too expensive."
- "You already have a LEGO set."
- "You'll lose the pieces in two days."
- "What's different about this one?"

Each concern required a carefully rehearsed counter.

Too expensive? I'd contribute from my allowance and promise not to ask for anything else for three months (negotiated scope and budget compromise).

Already have LEGO? Yes, but not one that is technically challenging (differentiation and value add).

Losing the pieces? I'd keep them in labeled boxes by color (resource management and risk mitigation).

What's different about this one? It teaches you how suspension systems work. (Total nonsense but delivered with full confidence.)

Honestly, it's a miracle I didn't start using phrases like "long-term ROI."

The Moment of Truth

Eventually, I got what every project manager dreams of hearing:

"We'll think about it."

That wasn't a yes. But it wasn't a no. It was a *maybe,* and *maybe* is where magic begins.

A few days later, after proving my dedication (read: repeating the campaign with slightly different wording at every opportunity), my mom walked in with a slightly oversized bag from the toy store.

The project was approved. The purchase order had been fulfilled. Delivery successful.

And just like that, I had unknowingly completed my **first end-to-end life project**:

- Objective set
- Resources and scope defined.
- Stakeholders managed.

- Risks addressed.
- Communication handled.
- Successful Execution
- Celebration earned.

That LEGO set? I built it in record time, took pictures of it, and showed it to everyone I could.
But the real satisfaction didn't come from the toy itself.

It came from knowing that I'd made something *happen*, from nothing. That I'd persuaded, planned, negotiated, and delivered.

I ran a full project at age seven.

Whether I realized it or not, that mindset had already taken root, and it would shape everything that came next.

2.2. Understanding Stakeholders at Age Seven

At seven years old, I didn't know the term *stakeholder*.
I didn't know that projects have *influencers*, *decision-makers*, or *gatekeepers*.
But I did know this:
If I wanted that LEGO, I needed my parents to say "yes."

And not just *any* yes, a *coordinated*, *aligned*, and ideally *guilt-free* yes.

What I didn't realize back then was that I was doing something that senior project managers and executives still struggle with today: **identifying stakeholders, understanding their influence, managing their expectations, and navigating their personalities.**

And I learned these lessons the hard way, one carefully timed pitch and one raised eyebrow at a time.

Two Key Stakeholders, Two Very Different Personas

Let's break it down:

🎯 **Stakeholder A: My Dad**

- Role: The *gatekeeper*. The *initial filter*. The *first line of defense*.

- Traits: Empathetic, practical, highly alert to manipulation tactics.
- Goals: Keeping me happy *while* keeping household expenses under control.
- Risk appetite: Moderate, will support a request if it feels "reasonable."
- Soft spots: Academic performance, polite behavior, and anything labeled "educational."
- Triggers: Over-the-top begging, tantrums, or attempts to make him choose between me and mom.

Stakeholder B: My Mom

- Role: The *final approver*. The *budget controller*. The *silent judge who weighs everything with a look*.
- Traits: Calm but assertive, financially disciplined, allergic to emotional persuasion.
- Goals: Long-term family financial stability, minimal waste, no clutter.
- Risk appetite: Low, she does not like surprises, vague benefits, or excessive spending.
- Soft spots: Evidence-based arguments, self-initiative, showing signs of "growing up.
- Triggers: Illogical reasoning, asking at the wrong time, acting entitled.

Looking back, that was basically a textbook stakeholder map.

The funny thing is, even at that young age, I *instinctively knew* how different their decision-making processes were. I knew I couldn't use the same approach for both. I couldn't copy-paste the same "ask" and expect it to land. This was instinctive stakeholder tailoring, well before I ever saw a RACI chart.

Emotional Intelligence on Training Wheels

Here's what I understood, even without knowing the terminology:

- My dad responded to *emotion*, but only when wrapped in logic.
- My mom responded to *logic*, but only when delivered calmly and respectfully.
- Both appreciated **effort**, and neither liked being cornered or pressured.

Therefore, I made adjustments.

With my dad, I started planting seeds early: "Did you see the toy Ahmet got? His mom says it really helps with focus."

I'd fold in how I'd "been trying really hard in school," and how this toy was "actually complicated, it's not one of those silly ones."

With my mom, I saved the full proposal for a moment of peace. I used phrases like, "I've been thinking about this for a while," or "I know it's a lot, but I could help pay for part of it." I even showed her the instruction booklet as if it were a technical manual.

Sound familiar?

I was doing stakeholder influence mapping purely by feel; no templates were required.

The Influence Web Was Bigger Than I Thought

What I also learned was that not all stakeholders are direct decision-makers.
Some are *influencers*.
Some are *observers*.
Some are *wild cards*.

For example:

- My older cousin, who had the same LEGO set? His bragging indirectly impacted my "business case."
- My teacher, who had once praised me for being detail-oriented? That quote suddenly found its way into my sales pitch.
- Even the store clerk, who gave a glowing mini speech about how "smart kids usually love this model," I filed that as testimonial evidence.

In project terms, this was **gathering stakeholder endorsements** to build perceived value.

The Alignment Strategy

In every project, getting your stakeholders aligned is make-or-break.
Too much resistance? The whole thing stalls.
One person nodding while another scowls? That's misalignment, and it's dangerous.

So, I staggered my approach:

1. **Test the waters with Stakeholder A (Dad).**
   - Present benefits. Gauge reaction.
   - Collect early support.

2. **Reinforce trust by demonstrating commitment.**
   - Clean my room. Finish homework. Volunteer to help.
   - Show I'm "maturing."

3. **Build the logical case for Stakeholder B (Mom).**
   - Emphasize effort, cost-sharing, and long-term value.
   - Time the conversation for maximum openness.

4. **Trigger the final alignment phase.**
   - Gently bring both parents together in a low-stress moment.
   - Present a united front: "Mom thinks it's a good idea, too."
   - Brace for the final verdict.

Spoiler alert: it worked.

But more importantly, it worked **because the approach was customized, timed, and emotionally intelligent**.

Realization in Hindsight

Looking back now with all the professional experience I've gained, it's honestly kind of amazing how natural this felt, even without knowing any of the theory. And it proves something I deeply believe:

We're all natural project managers; we just need to learn the language, sharpen the tools, and apply them intentionally.

That toy wasn't just a victory for my younger self.

It was the first time I realized that **people don't just respond to what you ask, they respond to how you ask, when you ask, and how you make them feel about saying yes**.

That insight?
It would become one of the most powerful tools in my adult life, far more useful than anything I learned from a textbook.

2.3. The First Mini Business Case: Making It Meaningful for Them

At seven years old, I didn't exactly walk into the living room with a PowerPoint deck and say, "Good evening, esteemed stakeholders. Please find my proposal for capital investment in cognitive development via targeted recreational enrichment."
But honestly?
That's basically what I was doing, just in kid language, pajamas, and a sugar rush of determination.

This was my **first attempt at building a business case**. I just didn't know it yet.

Because here's the thing:
When you really want something, and you know the people around you don't see it the same way, you have to **bridge the gap** between your desire and their perspective.

You have to make it meaningful for them, not to you.

The Core of Any Business Case: What's *in* It for Them?

When adults hear "business case," they often think of spreadsheets, ROI, and long-winded justifications that make people's eyes glaze over.

But at its core, a business case answers one simple question:

Why should they say yes?

That's it.

That's the question I needed to answer for my parents, each in their own way.

For my dad, the key decision factor was emotional logic. He didn't want me to be spoiled, but he didn't want to crush my spirit either. He needed to see:

- That I was learning something.
- That I appreciated the value.
- That I wouldn't toss the toy aside in 15 minutes.

Consequently, my business case for him focused on:

- Educational value: *"It improves my concentration!"*
- Personal growth: *"I want to challenge myself!"*
- Long-term engagement: *"This will take me days to build!"*

For my mom, the pitch needed to sound more like a return-on-investment conversation:

- Durability: *"It's not like those toys that break easily. It's really well-made."*
- Value: *"It has over 1,000 pieces!" (Implying 'price per piece' value, clever, right?)*
- Responsibility: *"I'll use my allowance to help pay for it."*

They weren't just parents. They were **two types of decision-makers**. And my job was to build a case that **answered both of their objections before they even voiced them**.

Visualizing the Pitch (Mentally, at Least)

I didn't have slides, but I had **talking points**, the kid version.

I anticipated their concern and crafted pre-emptive rebuttals:

Concern	My Counterargument
"It's too expensive."	"I'll use my allowance to help."
"You'll forget about it in a week."	"It'll take me days to build!"
"You already have a LEGO set."	"Yes, but that one's basic, this one is advanced."
"You're just copying your friends."	"I saw it before they did, actually."
"We can't buy toys all the time."	"This is the only one I want this year."

I was, unknowingly, doing what product managers do all the time: Anticipating objections and showing value from the stakeholder's point of view.

Tapping Into Values That Matter

One of the smartest things I did (and again, I had no clue how strategic this was) was to **tap into my parents' values**.

- They valued discipline. → I pointed out how I'd been helping around the house.
- They valued education. → I framed the toy as learning based.
- They valued patience → I emphasized the complexity of the build.
- They valued responsibility → I offered to co-finance it with my saved-up coins.

This was less about manipulation and more about empathy, **putting myself in their shoes** and speaking to what mattered to them, not just to me.

And that's what every good business case should do.

The Magic of Specificity

Here's something I learned early and still apply in my professional life today:

Vague = Dismissible. Specific = Believable.

Saying "I'll play with it" was weak. Saying "It has four modules to build, and I'll finish one each weekend" made it sound like a plan.

Saying "It's a good toy" felt empty. Saying "It teaches kids about how suspension systems work" (which, okay, might've been a bit of a stretch) made it sound scientific.

The more *specific* I got, the more they nodded.

Even now, when I coach project leads or help people build cases for getting budget or stakeholder buy-in, I say the same thing: **be specific. Ground your ask in something measurable, relatable, and real.**

I Didn't Just Want the Toy; I Made It Their Idea to Say Yes

The final layer of my mini business case?

I made it feel like **they were making the smart decision**, not caving to a child's request.

I had planted ideas like:

- "These are supposed to be great for kids who want to be engineers."
- "I read something about it in a school magazine..."
- "My teacher said I'm really good at focusing on details."

It was subtle, but powerful. I was giving them **reasons to feel good about saying yes**.

In corporate terms? I was increasing stakeholder buy-in by **aligning the project goals with their values** and making the decision look like a win-win.

And honestly? It worked.

Because within a week, that LEGO box was in my hands.

Final Thought

When people say, "kids can be so manipulative," what they really mean is that **kids are incredibly observant, emotionally intelligent, and capable of building instinctive strategies to get what they want**.

That's not manipulation. That's early-stage project leadership.

And the first time you write a business case, even without realizing it, is the first time you begin learning how to **lead with purpose, empathy, and persuasion**.

That lesson has stayed with me in every job, every negotiation, and every proposal I've made since.

And it all started with that LEGO set.

2.4. Executing the Plan and Celebrating the Win

After all the stakeholder analysis, emotional storytelling, and what I now recognize as a wildly successful business case for a seven-year-old, the moment finally arrived.

The LEGO Off-Road Car was in my hands.

I held the box like it was sacred. The weight. The design. The picture on the front shows the beast of a machine I would build with my own hands.

I wasn't just excited, I felt victorious.
But this wasn't the end of the story.

This was the **project execution time**.
And like any good project, **what comes after "yes" is just as important as how you got there**.

Step 1: Unboxing the Deliverables (Literally)

You know that moment when a project moves from proposal to action? That mobilization phase?

That's how it felt opening that LEGO box.

Hundreds of pieces. Multiple instruction booklets. Stickers, rods, and those weird little pivoting pieces that seemed useless, until you realize they're the linchpin of the entire build. It was overwhelming, but in the best way.

I laid everything out on the floor like a project manager organizing her resources for kickoff.
In my mind, I had already created a build schedule:

- Phase 1: Chassis
- Phase 2: Suspension and wheels
- Phase 3: Upper frame and aesthetic pieces
- Phase 4: Final assembly and sticker application
- Phase 5: Show it off to absolutely everyone within arm's reach.

Yes, I was *that* kid.

Step 2: Sticking to the Plan (With Some Scope Creep)

I was determined to follow the instruction booklet exactly.
No skipped steps. No shortcuts. Full compliance with the manufacturer's process.

And yet...

Halfway through, I decided the front winch would look cooler in a different position. Then I added some "customization," a spoiler built from leftover parts. At one point, I even paused the build to create a separate mini off-roader, just for fun, just because I could.

Classic **scope creep**.
But you know what? That's part of the real-world project experience. Even the best-laid plans need to allow space for creativity, improvisation, and adaptation when inspiration hits.

Sure, it wasn't 100% according to the original design. But it was *mine*. It still rolled beautifully. It still looked like a beast. And it still taught me something incredibly valuable:

Execution doesn't always mean rigid control; it means moving forward with clarity, flexibility, and ownership.

Step 3: Quality Assurance – Testing the Deliverable

Once it was built, I gave it a proper test run. Carpet? Smooth.
Table? A bit slippery.
My cousin? Equal parts impressed... and extremely jealous.

The toy worked just as I'd imagined, but better still, **it delivered on the promise I'd made to my parents**.

I didn't abandon it after two days.
I didn't lose the pieces.
And I definitely didn't stop talking about how it taught me "engineering skills" for at least three weeks (marketing never sleeps).

That's **post-project benefits realization**, folks.
Also known as: keeping your word after delivery.

Step 4: Celebrating the Win (and Learning to Reflect)

There's this thing in project management called a *retrospective*, it's where you take a moment after a project ends to ask:

- What went well?
- What could have gone better?
- What would we do differently next time?

Now, as a kid, I didn't do formal retrospectives. But I did something close.

I stared at that finished LEGO car and felt proud, not just of the build, but of the whole journey. The campaign. The careful planning. The patient negotiation. The execution.

And something inside me clicked:

"If I can make this happen... what else can I make happen?"

That was a powerful moment, one we often skip in adult life.
We move from one accomplishment to the next without stopping to appreciate the fact that we pulled something off. That we led something. That we delivered.

So, I celebrated. I showed the toy to my friends. I talked about the process. And I let myself feel proud, not just for building the LEGO car, but for **orchestrating the win** from start to finish.

Final Thought

Execution is where dreams get built and where lessons stick.
It's not always perfect. You improvise, you troubleshoot, you make weird adjustments that seemed like a good idea at the time.

But it's also where confidence is built.
Where your preparation meets reality.
Where the lessons really stick.

For seven-year-old me, this wasn't just about plastic bricks.
It was about realizing that with a little strategy, a bit of emotional intelligence, and a lot of patience, **you can make things happen**.

Even when you don't have the power... you still have influence.

Even when you don't have the authority... you can create momentum.

That lesson would follow me through school, jobs, relocations, career changes, health setbacks, and eventually writing this book.

And it all started with one toy, two parents, and a very determined kid with a plan.

2.5. Key Takeaways & Try This in Your Life

We've just explored one of life's most "innocent" projects, convincing your parents to buy you a toy.

But as you've seen, it was far from simple.

Beneath the surface of that childhood moment were the **seeds of real project management**, stakeholder engagement, persuasion, planning, execution, and reflection.

And whether you're seven, seventeen, or forty-seven, these lessons still hold true.

✅ Key Takeaways

1. Stakeholder Management Starts Early

Every project, no matter how personal or professional, involves people. People with different goals, fears, expectations, and decision-making styles. The sooner you understand who holds influence and how they think, the more effective you become at building trust and securing buy-in.

2. Tailor Your Message for Your Audience

What works for one person may not work for another. Your message needs to speak to the *values and motivations* of the person you're trying to convince. The same idea, framed differently, can be the difference between rejection and approval.

3. Timing is Everything

Even the best pitch can fall flat if delivered at the wrong moment. Emotional state, stress levels, and environmental context all matter. Good project managers know when to press forward and when to pause.

4. A Business Case Doesn't Need Flash, Just Relevance

You don't need slick decks or jargon. What matters is clarity: Why this? Why now? What value does it bring? Speak their language, not yours.

5. Execution Builds Confidence

Planning is powerful, but action is where belief is born. Following through, adapting mid-build, and delivering results all reinforce the idea that **you can make things happen**. That confidence will serve you for life.

6. Celebrate the Win, Then Reflect

So many of us achieve things and instantly move on. But every project, even small ones, has lessons to offer. Stop. Reflect. Celebrate. Then carry those lessons forward into the next project, and you'll be better for it.

🛠 Try This in Your Life

Let's take the insights from this chapter and turn them into an exercise you can use **today**.

🧠 Mini Project: Influence with Intention

Step 1: Identify a "yes" you're trying to get right now It could be:

- Asking for a raise or promotion.
- Convincing your partner to support a new goal.
- Pitching an idea to your team.
- Requesting mentorship.
- Negotiating a new opportunity.

Step 2: Map Your Stakeholders Ask yourself:

- Who is involved in this decision?
- What are their motivations?
- What are their concerns?
- What's their current mood/context?

Step 3: Create a Simple Business Case Write down:

- What's the value to them?
- What problem are you helping solve?
- How are you addressing their concerns?
- What's the right time/place to approach them?

Step 4: Pitch It with Empathy and Clarity Test it out. Observe the response. Be flexible. Adjust if needed.

Step 5: Reflect

- Did you prepare enough?
- How did it feel?
- What worked well?
- What would you do differently next time?

Even if it doesn't go perfectly, you're building a muscle.
One that will serve you every time you need to influence, inspire, or make a change happen.

Final Thought

Project management isn't just about charts and timelines.
It's about **understanding people, timing your efforts, and moving with purpose**.

If a seven-year-old can use these tools to turn a "no" into a LEGO masterpiece... just imagine what you could do with a bit more intention in your everyday life.

The principles are timeless.
The impact? Entirely up to you.

Bonus Visual: Stakeholder Map: My First Project Plan

Even as a kid, I was doing stakeholder analysis without knowing it. This map breaks down how I approached my two key decision-makers with completely different styles. It turns out, persuasion is all about speaking the right language to the right person.

Mom - Final Approver
Traits: Caring values effort and logic
Influence: High
Soft Spot: Academic performance, emotional appeal

Dad- Gatekeeper
Traits: Pragmatic, risk-averse, disciplined
Influence: Medium
Soft Spot: Well-structured arguments, calm tone

CHAPTER 03

Navigating Life Alone

"Out of suffering have emerged the strongest souls; the most massive characters are seared with scars."
—Khalil Gibran

3.1. When Childhood Ends Too Early

There's a moment in every person's life when everything changes.

Sometimes it's a slow burn, barely noticeable until you look back and realize how far you've drifted from who you were.
And sometimes, it's instant.

For me, it was the second kind.

I was 11 years old. My mom, who had been battling health issues, passed away suddenly in her sleep. Heart failure. She was 37. Thirty-seven.

She wasn't elderly. She wasn't at the end of some long medical journey. She was just... gone. Overnight.

I still remember that day, not as a memory, but as a fracture: a clean break between *before* and *after*.

One moment, I was a boy with a mother.
Next, I was a boy navigating a world that suddenly felt unsafe, unkind, and completely out of my control.

There are no blueprints for grief at that age.
No handbooks. No structured curriculum for how to process loss, especially when your brain hasn't even mastered long division.

All I knew was that something massive had been ripped away, and nothing made sense anymore.

The World Doesn't Pause for Grief

The next few weeks were a blur, relatives coming and going, friends who didn't know what to say, teachers trying to be kind but never quite getting it right.

Meanwhile, life went on. School went on. Expectations remained.

And I learned something early: **life doesn't wait for you to catch up.**
When your world stops spinning, everyone else keeps going.

I was scared.
I was angry.
And I was lost.

But I also knew I couldn't afford to fall apart.

Not because I was brave. But because I didn't have a choice.

Enter: My Second Family

My father was battling his own demons. Alcohol had been a problem for years, and after my mom's death, it became harder for him to function. He wasn't in a place to raise a grieving child. Not emotionally. Not practically.

That's when my uncle and grandparents stepped in.

They didn't just give me a home, they gave me structure.
They didn't just provide food and clothes, they offered unconditional support.

My uncle, in particular, became a quiet hero in my life. He was never loud, never dramatic, but he showed up. Every single day.
And my grandparents? They treated me like their own son. I was never a burden to them, though I sometimes feared I was.

They **didn't give me my old life back**, but they gave me something else: a new foundation.

And looking back, that's when I started building the internal tools I'd use for the rest of my life.

Tools I now recognize as project management skills, though back then, I had no name for them.

My First Solo Project: Emotional Survival

There's no Gantt chart for grief.
No stakeholder alignment when the primary stakeholder is gone.

But even then, I started doing something instinctively, something that I've come to see as a personal *project charter for survival*:

- **Objective:** Stay grounded. Keep going. Don't collapse.
- **Resources:** My grandparents. My uncle. My friends. School. Books. Hope.
- **Constraints:** Grief. Uncertainty. Emotional fatigue.
- **Risks:** Shutting down. Losing motivation. Falling behind in life.
- **Timeline:** Unknown.
- **Success criteria:** I didn't know it then, but it was simply "keep moving forward."

I began creating little rituals to anchor myself.

Waking up at the same time each day.
Doing my homework with military precision.
Reading books, because in books, no one you love disappears between chapters.

Studying hard because good grades gave me some illusion of control.

What I now understand is that I was creating **systems**, tiny project management processes, to **cope with chaos**.

Structure gave me stability.
Goals gave me purpose.
Discipline gave me something to cling to when emotions felt too big to hold.

What I Didn't Realize Then

I was building **resilience as a system**.

Not by reading about it.
Not by listening to motivational speeches.
But by surviving one day at a time, using **whatever tools I had**, routine, effort, planning, and people.

And in doing so, I laid the foundation for how I'd approach everything in my life after that.

Because once you've been through something like that, you learn to:

- **Scan for risks before they hit.**
- **Identify your allies early.**
- **Hold onto structure when everything else feels unstable.**
- **Break big problems into small, manageable parts.**
- **Find your *why*, because otherwise, you'll drown in *what*.**

I wouldn't have called myself a project manager at 11.
But in hindsight? I was leading a project with the highest stakes imaginable: **my own ability to keep living after loss.**

3.2. Creating Structure When the World Felt Unstable

After my mother passed away, the world didn't just feel sad, it felt unstable.
Everything I once counted on felt rearranged.
Nothing felt solid.
Nothing made sense.

And when you're a child who's used to having a "safe place," someone to hug you, remind you to brush your teeth, ask how your day went, and suddenly that person disappears, it's like waking up in a new dimension. One where the rules haven't been explained yet, but the consequences are very real.

In that strange new world, I discovered something unexpected:
I needed structure.

Not because I was naturally organized (I wasn't).
Not because someone told me to (no one did).
But without it, I could feel myself slipping.

Structure became the **invisible scaffolding** holding me up while I rebuilt myself.

🧱 Rituals Were My First Building Blocks

It started with small things.

Waking up at the same time each morning.
Laying out my clothes the night before.
Arranging my schoolbooks by subject and checking them twice before leaving home.
Reading the same comics, in the same order, every Sunday morning.

On the surface, it looked like a kid just trying to be more independent.
But inside, these rituals were my **early risk control mechanisms**.
They were helping me reduce the **emotional volatility** that grief and uncertainty created.

It turns out, this was my first experience with a concept I'd later use in every major project:

Stability through repeatable systems.

Just like projects thrive with predictable workflows, I began to thrive when I gave myself simple, repeatable actions that made life feel less chaotic.

🧭 When You Can't Control the Big Things, Master the Small Ones

I couldn't bring my mother back.
I couldn't heal my father.

I couldn't stop the well-meaning adults around me from awkwardly trying to cheer me up or offering advice that didn't help.

But I could **do my homework with precision**.
I could **organize my drawers, my bag, and my desk**.
I could **set goals** for my next exam or try to memorize a full poem ahead of class.

Was it obsessive? Maybe a little.

But that focus gave me tiny wins, and those wins kept the darkness at bay.

These small victories were my version of **micro-deliverables**.
And each one, no matter how small, helped me maintain momentum when my heart wanted to shut down.

📊 How I Learned to Manage Emotional Risks

In professional project management, we talk a lot about **risk identification and mitigation**.
We do it with stakeholders, budgets, tech dependencies, but rarely with our inner selves.

Yet, during those early years, I was managing **emotional risk** every day.

I knew certain conversations or places could trigger me.
So I avoided them, or prepared mentally beforehand.
I learned to sense when I was spiraling into anger or sadness, and I would **interrupt the pattern** by focusing on something I could control, like solving a math problem or organizing my books.

I didn't know it then, but this was **risk response planning** in action:

Trigger	Response Strategy
Sudden memory of my mom	Shift focus to a mental task (reading, solving)
Feeling invisible at school	Engage in a classroom question to re-anchor
Loneliness	Spend extra time with grandparents, my uncle, or friends.

This wasn't about avoiding feelings. It was about **not being consumed by them**.

And honestly? That's a skill many adults are still learning.

Creating Meaning in the Midst of the Mess

Looking back, I think part of what made structure so powerful for me during that time was that it helped me find **a sense of meaning**, even when life felt unfair.

I couldn't change what had happened.

But I could decide how I showed up.
I could decide that **I wouldn't be the kid who gave up**.
I wouldn't become bitter.
I wouldn't let grief define me.

I'd find meaning in action.
And, meaning, in project language, is called **purpose**.

Every time I stuck to my little rituals, or studied hard for a test, or helped my grandparents without being asked, I was reinforcing that purpose.

It was like I was saying to life:

"You may have knocked me down, but I'm still here, and I've got a plan."

The First Life Framework

So many years later, I realized I had created my own **resilience framework** without knowing it. Something like this:

1. **Create Daily Structure** → Routine equals safety.
2. **Focus on Small Wins** → Accomplishments fuel hope.
3. **Know Your Triggers** → Awareness is the first step to healing.
4. **Have a Support System** → You don't need to do it all alone.
5. **Redefine Control** → When the big things are broken, master the small ones.
6. **Keep Moving Forward** → Even slow progress is still progress.

That framework didn't come from a book. It came from pain, survival, and a little boy doing his best not to fall apart.

And while I wouldn't wish that experience on anyone, I can honestly say:
It made me stronger.
It made me more self-aware.

And it gave me tools that would serve me again and again, in exams, career changes, relationships, burnout, and building a future from scratch.

3.3. Lessons in Resilience: Grief as a Risk Factor

At some point, I realized grief wasn't something that faded; it just changed form.

Some days it showed up quietly, like a memory.
Other days, it hit me like a tidal wave out of nowhere, triggered by a smell, a sound, or even the sudden silence in a room.

I've worked on high-risk projects since then, multi-million-euro programs with tight deadlines, complex dependencies, and demanding stakeholders, but let me tell you something:

Grief is the first high-impact risk I ever had to manage.

And no one taught me how to do it.
There were no templates.
No process documents.
No seasoned PM whispering, "Here's how you manage losing the person who was your entire world."

I had to figure it out, piece by piece.

💔 Understanding Grief as a Life Risk

In traditional project language, a risk is anything that could threaten your objectives. Something that might delay the schedule, increase costs, or throw the team off course.

Grief? It does all of that, and more.

- It disrupts **motivation**.
- It impairs **focus**.
- It unleashes **emotional volatility**.
- It leads to **withdrawal**, loss of communication, and sometimes even shutdown.

If I were to write a risk log from that time in my life, it would've looked something like this:

Risk	Probability	Impact	Mitigation Strategy
Loss of emotional stability	High	High	Stick to structured routines
Academic underperformance	Medium	High	Daily study goals + support from teachers
Isolation from friends	Medium	Medium	Force social interaction through safe channels
Unprocessed grief becomes depression.	High	High	Stay close to trusted adults and friends and share feelings
Disruption in the home environment	Medium	High	Build an emotional connection with caregivers

Did I actually write this down at the time? Of course not.
But now, looking back, I can see how much I was already thinking in those terms.
I was identifying threats and adjusting my behavior, subconsciously creating a **risk management mindset for my emotional life**.

🧠 From Survival to Strategy

Surviving grief as a child did something permanent to my brain: it made me learn how to **prepare for the worst without becoming paralyzed by it**.

It's a skill I've used in every major challenge since.

- When a key stakeholder suddenly quits on a project.
- When I had to pivot a career path after years of commitment.
- When I faced burnout in a toxic job, I had to rebuild from the ground up.

In all of those situations, I instinctively applied the same thinking I used back when I was 11:

"What's the worst-case scenario? Can I prepare for it? Can I recover from it?"

That mental rehearsal, that risk planning, it didn't make me pessimistic.
It made me *resilient*.

I'd already seen what it looks like when the bottom falls out, and I knew I could rebuild, even from scratch.

Building the Muscle of Mental Resilience

People often romanticize resilience, like it's some kind of superhero trait. But the truth is, it's often quiet. Unseen. Unapplaud.

It's getting out of bed when you'd rather stay curled under the blanket of grief.
It's showing up to school and sitting through classes while your mind drifts back to what you've lost.
It's answering "I'm fine" when you're not, just to make it through the moment.

But over time, those quiet micro-decisions add up, and that's how resilience is built.
Resilience isn't built in one grand act, but it's forged in a hundred quiet moments.

In project terms, it's like **delivering a little value in every sprint**, even when your team is running on fumes.
It's choosing progress over perfection, and **forward motion over emotional inertia**.

That's what I did. And that's what I still do.

The Most Personal Risk Register I Ever Carried

For a long time, I didn't talk about these things.
Because in most cultures, especially back then, boys were expected to be "strong."
And strong often meant silent.

But here's the truth I learned the hard way:

Grief doesn't shrink when you ignore it. It grows roots.

You have to name it. Face it.
Sometimes you even have to plan around it, like a project manager planning around bad weather or budget cuts.

It's not a weakness. It's wisdom.

And now, in every big life decision I make, whether moving to another country, starting a new job, or writing a book, I still use that same mindset:

- Where could this hurt?
- How do I prepare?
- Who can I lean on?
- What resources do I already have?

That's risk planning.
But more importantly, it's self-care and project management style.

3.4. Finding Support Systems: Every Project Needs a Team

If grief taught me that life is unpredictable, then my uncle, grandparents, and close friends taught me something even more powerful:

You don't have to do it all alone.

Even though I felt alone after my mom passed, I wasn't. Not really. I just didn't realize how much of a team had quietly formed around me.

They didn't wear capes or use inspirational speeches
They didn't promise to fix everything.
They didn't even always know what to say.

But they were there.
Every day.
In the background.
Holding me together, piece by piece.

👵👨 The Quiet Heroes of My Life

My **uncle** didn't lecture me. He didn't try to be a replacement father. But he showed up. Constantly.

He was dependable, kind, and present, three qualities I now realize are rarer than they should be.

He took on responsibilities without complaint. He encouraged me when I needed it. And perhaps most importantly, he let me grieve in my own way without pushing me to "get over it."

My **grandparents** treated me as their own.
I was never made to feel like an outsider.
They created routines. They made sure I had food, clothes, and a warm bed. They gave me the kind of emotional grounding that many project managers spend years trying to give their teams **a sense of psychological safety**.

No judgment.
No pressure to "perform."
Just love, structure, and consistency.

And then, there were my close friends.

Not always the loudest voices, not always the ones with the "perfect" words, but they were there. Some of them probably didn't even know what I was going through in detail, but they instinctively knew how to bring light into dark moments. Whether it was cracking a joke during a heavy day, inviting me into their homes without making me feel like "the kid who lost his mom," or just treating me normally when all I wanted was a sliver of normality, **those small gestures meant more than they'll ever know**.

In the quiet background of my grief, they became part of my first real tribe. They reminded me, without even trying, that life could still be joyful, messy, and shared. That I wasn't alone in the world, even if it felt that way sometimes. For that, I'll be forever grateful.

👥 Why Every Life (and Project) Needs a Support System

In the project world, we build support systems all the time:

- Steering committees
- Project sponsors
- Escalation paths
- Cross-functional teams

We do this because **even the best project manager can't do everything alone**.

You need people who can spot what you can't.

Who brings strengths you don't have?
Those who believe in the outcome, even when progress is slow.

In life, it's no different.

And back then, **my uncle, grandparents, and close friends were my project sponsors and the core team.**
They believed in me before I believed in myself.
They stepped in to fill roles I didn't know I needed:

- Emotional resilience officers
- Logistics coordinators
- Budget controllers
- Spiritual advisors (my grandma prayed for me like I was running for presidency)

They were **my first true team**, and without them, I honestly don't know where I would've ended up.

🧠 Project Lesson: Build Your Team Intentionally

One of the hardest truths I've learned is that **not everyone deserves a seat at your project table**.

Sometimes, when we're hurt, we try to please everyone.
We let the wrong people in, thinking we need their approval
We confuse proximity with support.
We mistake attention for loyalty.

But here's the deal:
In projects, we only assign roles to people who contribute to success.
Why should life be any different?

Back then, I didn't choose my support system, but I was **extremely lucky** to land in the care of people who genuinely had my back.

Now, as an adult, I apply that lesson with full intention.
Whether I'm building a team at work, choosing mentors, or even just deciding who I call when things go sideways, I ask myself:

- Does this person support my growth?
- Do they show up when it matters?

- Do they make things clearer or more confusing?
- Do I feel safe being vulnerable around them?

If the answer is no, they're not on the team.

What Support Looks Like Isn't Always Obvious

Sometimes, support is a hug.
Other times, it's a plate of warm food left quietly on the table.
Or a look across the room that says, "You've got this."

And as I've grown older, I've realized that **support isn't about fixing, it's about holding space**.

That's what my family and friends did for me.
They didn't erase the pain.
They gave it a place to sit without judgment and helped me find a way forward despite it.

And now, when I lead teams or mentor others, I try to offer that same type of space.

Sometimes, what someone needs isn't more advice or more productivity tools.
They just need to know they're not carrying it all alone.

The People Who Lifted the Project

If my life were a project in its early crisis phase, my uncle, grandparents, and close friends were the **stabilizing task force** that kept it from collapsing.

They gave me:

- **Consistency** when everything felt unstable.
- **Encouragement** when I doubt myself.
- **Boundaries** that made me feel safe.
- **Patience** when I was angry, silent, or sad.
- **Belief** that I still had a future worth fighting for

Their influence shows up in every part of who I am today, in how I lead, how I love, and how I think.

And that's why I'll say this to anyone navigating hard seasons in life:

Don't manage the project alone. Build your support system like your dream team: with care, trust, and purpose.

3.5. Key Takeaways & Try This in Your Life

This chapter wasn't about traditional success.
It wasn't about climbing the ladder, hitting milestones, or delivering some breakthrough result.

It was about **survival**.
It was about **growing up too soon**
It was about finding order in chaos and doing it in a way that builds something no one can take from you: resilience.

Let's pull the key lessons together.

✅ Key Takeaways

1. Grief Is a High-Impact Risk, But It Can Be Managed
It may never fully disappear, but it can be acknowledged, planned around, and softened with structure, purpose, and support.

2. Structure Creates Stability in Unstable Times
Daily rituals, checklists, and routines might seem small, but they're powerful tools when everything else feels out of control.

3. Pain Is a Brutal but Brilliant Teacher
The darkest moments often plant the seeds of the strongest skills. Pain sharpened your awareness. It forced you to listen, adapt, and build systems for staying afloat.

4. No Project Should Be Done Alone

Whether you call them family, friends, mentors, or community, every life project needs a team. Lean on them, thank them, and choose them wisely.

5. Resilience Is a System You Build Over Time

It's not one grand comeback. It's dozens of small decisions, made consistently, even when you don't feel strong. Especially then.

🛠 Try This in Your Life

🔍 Your Personal Resilience Map

Take 10–15 minutes to reflect and build your own mini framework for resilience, using these prompts:

Step 1: Identify Your Emotional Anchors

- What habits or routines help you feel grounded when things feel overwhelming?
- List 3 small rituals that give your day structure or stability.

Step 2: List Your Support Team

- Who do you turn to when life gets tough? Who checks in on you without being asked?
- Write down 3 people who have supported you, and what role they play (cheerleader, listener, advisor, etc.).

Step 3: Spot Your Inner Risks

- What emotional or mental "triggers" tend to knock you off track?
- What helps you get back on track when that happens?

Step 4: Define One "Win" Worth Celebrating

- Think of a time you got through something tough, even if it didn't feel heroic at the time.
- What did you learn from it? What inner strength did you use?

You don't need to be in crisis to build resilience.
You can prepare now, reflect now, and **design a system for strength before the storm hits**.

🧠 Final Thought

You didn't choose the loss
You didn't choose the pain.
But you can choose to keep going. To rebuild. To rise.

And that, in every sense of the word, is **project leadership at its rawest and most powerful**.

Some projects don't have formal kick-offs.

Some begin with silence.
Some begin with heartbreak.

But what matters is that you take the lead anyway, and start shaping your life with one decision, one day, one breath at a time.

Bonus Tool: Personal Risk Register for a Grief & Resilience Project

Risk Description	Probability	Impact	Response Strategy
Emotional instability (grief waves)	High	High	Daily structure, journaling, and focused routines
Academic underperformance	Medium	High	Clear study plan, self-set goals, and extra tutoring support
Social withdrawal/ isolation	Medium	Medium	Proactive engagement with friends & school activities
Loss of motivation	Medium	High	Celebrate small wins, stay connected to long-term goals
Feeling like a burden to caregivers	Medium	Medium	Honest conversations with family, gratitude expression
Unprocessed grief turning into depression.	High	High	Regular emotional check-ins, reading, and seeking safe spaces
Fear of uncertainty or the future	High	Medium	Focus on what's controllable, set short-term milestones

How to Use This Tool

You can't "solve" grief, but you can prepare for the emotional storms that come with it. This simple **risk register** helped me (without realizing it at the time) identify what could derail me and gave me tools to keep moving forward.

You can use the same concept in your own life, especially when navigating loss, burnout, or uncertain transitions. Awareness is half the battle; **the moment you name a risk, you start to reclaim your power over it.**

CHAPTER 04

The Exam Mission: Studying for the University Entrance Like a Real Project

"Success is the sum of small efforts, repeated day in and day out."
—Robert Collier

4.1. The Exam That Could Define Everything

If you grew up in a country like Turkey, then you already know what I'm about to say.
If you didn't, let me paint the picture for you.

There's an exam. A monster of a thing.
The *university entrance exam*, or as we called it, the ÖSS (or later YGS/LYS, depending on the year you took it).
And for millions of students, it's not just a test.
It's a national ritual. A psychological pressure cooker. A career GPS. A factory of family expectations.

A cocktail of pride, shame, stress, hope, and identity, compressed into a ticking multiple-choice booklet.

No pressure, right?

It's the kind of exam that determines **which university you'll go to**, which often influences **what job you'll get**, which may ultimately shape **who people think you are**.

In short, **this exam could define everything.**

And in my case, I knew from the start that I didn't have the luxury of messing it up.

When You Don't Have a Backup Plan

I didn't come from a background where "trying again next year" felt like a real option.
There wasn't a safety net waiting to catch me if I failed.

I had lost my parents.
I was already living with my uncle and grandparents, grateful, but determined not to become a "burden."
This exam wasn't just about getting into a good school. It was about **proving to myself and the world that I could build a future, even if life had thrown me off-course early.**

I needed to get it right.
Not perfect, but *right enough* to unlock doors.

That's when I made the decision that changed everything:

I was going to treat the university entrance exam as a full-blown project.

Not a wish. Not a hope.
A project with structure, goals, milestones, risks, backups, and a post-launch evaluation.

Turning a Vague Goal into a Concrete Plan

At first, the goal was fuzzy:
"Get into a good university."
But vague goals don't lead to clear results.
Good project managers don't work with vague goals; they **define success**.

So, I asked myself:

- *Which university do I want to get into?*
- *Which department?*
- *What score range do I need?*
- *How many questions can I afford to miss?*
- *What are my weakest areas right now?*

Suddenly, this overwhelming mountain began to look like a map.
Still scary, but now I could see the path.

And let me tell you, **creating a study plan felt a lot like creating a project work breakdown structure (WBS)**, though I had no clue what that was at the time.

🧠 My Mindset Shift: From Student to Project Manager

Here's what changed for me:

- I stopped thinking like a student cramming for a test.
- I started thinking like a **leader delivering a mission-critical launch.**

I set goals. I created a timetable. I built in buffers for revision and mock exams.
I tracked my progress like a KPI dashboard.
I took breaks like strategic downtime to avoid burnout.
I had a notebook where I logged weak spots (my personal "issue log").

I wasn't just reacting to stress anymore; I was managing it.
And in that shift, I uncovered one of the most important lessons of my life:

Clarity kills anxiety. Structure creates confidence.

The more I planned, the less overwhelmed I felt.
Not because the task got smaller, but because **I got stronger**.

📅 My Study Project Charter (Even If I Didn't Call It That)

Let's be honest, I wasn't walking around at 16 calling things "charters." But if I had to recreate it today, it would look something like this:

Project Title	University Entrance Master Plan
Objective	Achieve the required score to enter the target university & department.
Timeline	24 months
Key Deliverables	Mastery of math, science, Turkish, and social studies
Milestones	Monthly mock exams, 4-hour study blocks, periodic self-assessments
Risks	Burnout, loss of motivation, gaps in weak subjects
Mitigation	Balanced study plan, breaks, study group, and teacher feedback

Stakeholders	Myself, my family, my future
Success Criteria	Secure a placement within the top 5,000 out of 3 million nationwide candidates.

Even though I didn't write it this way at the time, the spirit of it was there.
I was operating with purpose.
And more than that, I was no longer at the mercy of the exam.

I was managing the exam.

4.2. Building a Real Study Plan: WBS, Timeboxes, and Mock Exams

There's this moment in every high-stakes project where panic tries to take over.

You've defined your goal. You understand what's at stake.
But then you look at the sheer size of the work ahead of you, and you feel that tiny voice in your head whispering:

"This is too much. There's no way you can handle all this."

And honestly? That voice had a point.
Try to eat the whole elephant at once, and you'll choke.

So instead of letting that overwhelm paralyze me, I did the only thing that made sense:
I broke the whole thing down.

That's when I unknowingly created my first **Work Breakdown Structure**, though back then, I just called it "my epic study plan."

Breaking the Beast into Boxes: My First WBS

I had four core subjects to master:

- Math
- Science
- Turkish
- Social Studies (a.k.a. "everything else")

Naturally, I started by listing all the chapters and topics within each subject. Then I broke those down into subtopics. Then sub-sub-topics.

Suddenly, instead of a scary monolithic "Study Physics" task, I had a list that looked like this:

- Physics
    - Mechanics
        - Newton's Laws
        - Motion Equations
        - Inclined Planes & Friction
    - Electricity
        - Ohm's Law
        - Circuits
        - Resistors
    - Optics
        - Lenses & Mirrors
        - Refraction & Reflection

Each bullet point was a **manageable unit** of study.
Each unit was doable in a focused session or two.
Each completion gave me a little dopamine hit and a boost in confidence.

That was the magic:

When you break a mountain into pebbles, you can carry them one at a time.

⏳ Timeboxing and Sprints (Before I Knew What Agile Was)

Once I had my study tasks broken down, the next challenge was figuring out how to make time for them all.
Spoiler alert: you can't. Not all at once.

So, I created weekly sprints, my own version of study iterations.

Each week had:

- 4 days of deep study sessions (with two subjects per day)
- 1 day for review and mock exams
- 1 day for "backup topics" or catch-up
- And yes, **one full day off** to protect my sanity.

Within each day, I worked in **2-hour timeboxes**, something I had no name for at the time, but would later recognize as one of the most powerful tools in time and energy management.

I didn't wait to "feel ready" to study. I followed the timebox.

I'd tell myself:

"No distractions for 2 hours. After that, you can have a break, snack, or call your friend. But for these 2 hours, this is your mission."

That discipline became a habit, and that habit built the momentum.

🎯 Tracking Progress Like a KPI Dashboard

Every great project needs a way to measure success along the way, not just at the end.

That's why I created a **mock exam routine**:
One full-length practice test every month.

This gave me:

- A benchmark for performance
- A stress test under real conditions
- An emotional rehearsal for the real exam
- And honestly... a monthly reality check (because sometimes I felt confident, until the test told a different story)

Each score became a **data point**, not a judgment.
I used them to adjust my study plan:

- More time on weak areas
- Faster review of strong topics
- Repetition where I made consistent mistakes.

This was real-time feedback. It turned my plan into a living system.
It made me feel like I was leading the project, not being dragged by it.

🧠 What This Taught Me About Self-Leadership

Looking back now, I see how powerful this process was, not just for passing an exam, but for shaping the way I work and think.

I learned that:

- **A big goal without a breakdown is just anxiety in disguise.**
- **Big dreams only happen through small, consistent actions.**
- **Progress isn't linear, and that's okay.**
- **Discipline beats motivation every single time.**

Most importantly:

Project success is about showing up, not once, but again, and again, and again.

4.3. Discipline Over Motivation: Showing Up on the Hard Days

If there's one thing I learned from preparing for the university entrance exam, one truth that's followed me through relocations, career changes, book writing, and even healing my health, it's this:

Motivation is a luxury. Discipline is a necessity.

Motivation is great when it shows up.
It's exciting. Uplifting.
It gives you that boost of "I'm going to crush this!" energy.

But here's the truth: **it doesn't always show up.**

Some days you feel flat.
Some days you're tired.
Some days, the world feels heavy for no clear reason.
And yet... the work still has to be done.

That's when discipline steps in, not as punishment, but as a gift you give to your future self.

📅 When Motivation Was Missing

During those intense months of preparation, I had countless days when I just didn't feel like studying.

- Days when my brain felt foggy.
- Days when my mock exam score had dropped, and I was questioning whether I was even cut out for this.
- Days when I looked at my friends going out while I was reviewing problem sets on electricity... for the fourth time.
- Days when I remembered my mom wasn't around to cheer me on, and suddenly, everything felt heavier.

If I had relied on motivation alone, I would've quit dozens of times.

But instead, I relied on something stronger: **discipline built through structure**.

🧱 Discipline Is Built, Not Born

Discipline isn't something you're born with; it's something you design.

And during that exam prep, I unknowingly developed a few techniques that helped me **show up, even on the hard days**:

1. Timeboxing Was My Lifeline

I didn't say, "I'll study when I feel ready."
I said, "I'll study from 14:00 to 16:00, no matter what."

Whether I was in the mood or not didn't matter.
I just had to start.
And most days, once I got started, the resistance disappeared on its own.

2. I Focused on Progress, Not Perfection

I told myself:
"You don't need to study *everything* today. You just need to study *something*."

Even 45 minutes of good focus on one topic was a win.
One formula understood. One type of question is mastered.
It all added up.

3. I Designed My Environment for Success

My study corner became sacred. Clean desk. No phone. Fresh black tea. A small calendar where I could mark off days, I completed my targets.

That visual progress became a mini dopamine hit. A scoreboard that told me: "You're doing the work. You're getting there."

How I Dealt with Low-Energy Days

Some days, even with structure and good intentions, the engine sputtered.

Here's what helped me:

- **I scaled down without giving up.** If I couldn't do a full 2-hour session, I did 30 minutes and reviewed flashcards. It wasn't ideal, but it was something. And something was better than nothing.
- **I reviewed old wins.** I kept a few mock exams where I'd performed well. On bad days, I'd flip through them to remind myself: "You've done this before. You can do it again."
- **I used "habit stacking."** I tied my study sessions to everyday actions, like "After lunch, I always do physics," or "After my black tea, I open my math notebook." No debate. Just rhythm.

This created what I now know as **momentum loops**:
Start small → feel good → keep going → build confidence → repeat.

The Surprising Power of Lowering the Bar (Temporarily)

I remember one day, I was completely drained. No brainpower. No emotional energy.
I stared at my physics book like it had personally insulted me.

So, I did something strange: I gave myself permission to "study badly."

I said:

"You don't have to crush it today. Just sit here for 25 minutes and read one topic. Even if it doesn't fully stick, it still counts."

That tiny shift took the pressure off.
I wasn't chasing perfection; I was chasing presence.

And funny enough, after 10 minutes, I got into the flow anyway.

That's when I realized:

Discipline isn't about forcing greatness; it's about honoring the effort to show up.

📊 What This Taught Me About Leading Myself

Years later, while leading projects and teams, I saw the same truth:

- Everyone's motivated on Day 1.
- But projects aren't won on Day 1, they're won in the middle.
- The messy middle. The grind. The "I don't want to do this today" phase.

And the teams who win aren't the most talented.
They're the ones with **rituals, habits, systems, and accountability.**

Just like that 17-year-old kid in his room, checking off topics one by one.

4.4. Exam Day: Delivering the Project

After months of prep, mock exams, self-pep-talks, and enough pencil sharpening to decimate a forest... it was here.

Exam day.

The culmination of what had become the biggest personal project of my life up to that point.

And let me tell you, no matter how well-prepared you think you are, the night before a major exam hits differently.

😵‍💫 The Night Before: A Cocktail of Emotions

I went to bed early, but sleep? Not so much.
My brain decided it was a great time to replay every mock exam mistake I'd ever made.
A highlight reel of "What if you forget everything?" featuring a guest appearance from "Why didn't you study one more topic?"

I had done the work.
I had stuck to the plan.
But now, my biggest challenge wasn't the exam itself, it was **calming my own mind**.

That's when I reached for what every project manager does before a big launch: **a final pre-execution checklist.**

I checked my bag:
✅ ID
✅ Pencils and erasers
✅ Water bottle
✅ Printed exam entry document, double-checked, because my brain didn't trust me.

My own form of pre-launch quality control.
I wasn't leaving success to chance.

🏫 Arriving at the Exam Center – The War Room Vibes

Walking into the exam center felt like entering a control room before launch.

Everyone was quiet. Nervous. Focused.
Some were flipping through notes like they could download three chapters in five minutes.
Others sat completely still, eyes closed, breathing like monks.

I took a deep breath. Sat down.
And reminded myself:

"This is just another milestone. You've delivered every sprint. Now it's go time."

In that moment, I mentally stepped into **execution mode**.
No more prep. No more doubt.
Just focus. Presence. Delivery.

⌛ Time Management Under Pressure

The exam itself was 3 hours long, hours of reading, calculating, bubbling, double-checking, pacing yourself, and trying not to spiral when you hit a question that looked like it came from another dimension.

But because of the mock exams I'd done every single month for the last 2 years, I had a strategy:

- I divided the exam into **timeboxes**.
- I allotted a fixed number of minutes per section, with a small buffer at the end.
- If I got stuck, I moved on. No emotional attachment.
- I marked questions for review and circled back efficiently.

This was **an agile exam-taking**.
Iterative. Measured. Adaptive.

And even when the anxiety crept in, because of course it did, I used micro rituals to reset:

- Deep breath.
- Roll shoulders.
- Reread the question slowly.
- Visualize success.

In that moment, I wasn't just answering questions. I was delivering a project milestone that mattered.

Recovery and Post-Mortem

When the time was up, I walked out with a strange mix of exhaustion and release.

Did I feel like I aced it? Not entirely.

Did I feel like I had done my best? Absolutely.

And that was the real win.
Not perfection. Not having every answer.
But **knowing I had shown up fully prepared, fully present, and fully committed.**

That evening, I didn't touch a book.
I didn't analyze answers or refresh internet forums obsessively.
Instead, I gave myself permission to **breathe**, to celebrate the journey, and to rest.

Because in projects, success isn't just about the outcome, **it's about how well you executed with what you had.**

🧠 **What I Took from That Day**

- That performance under pressure comes from practice under pressure.
- That rituals and structure aren't just for study, they're for composure.
- That execution is its own skill, one that lives in the body, not just the brain.
- That's *how* you show up matters just as much as what you know.

And perhaps most importantly:

The biggest test isn't always what's in front of you; it's how you respond to it.

4.5. Key Takeaways & Try This in Your Life

The university entrance exam wasn't just about knowledge; it tested strategy, consistency, resilience, and execution under pressure.

In hindsight, it was the first time I applied the **full project management lifecycle** to something deeply personal, with stakes that felt sky-high.

I wasn't just trying to get a score.
I was building a future.
And project thinking helped me do it with clarity, confidence, and purpose.

✅ **Key Takeaways**

1. Break Big Goals into Smaller, Clear Tasks

When the goal feels overwhelming, zoom in. Break it down. Create your own Work Breakdown Structure (WBS). Small wins stack into big victories.

2. Timeboxing Beats To-Do Lists

Don't just list what you want to do, block out when and for how long. Set intentional start-and-stop boundaries. Timeboxing creates focus and flow.

3. Mock the Real Thing

Run simulations, practice under real conditions, and pressure-test yourself. It builds confidence and reveals weak spots early when they're still fixable.

4. Discipline > Motivation

Motivation comes and goes. Discipline keeps showing up. Systems win when willpower runs out.

5. Execution Is a Skill

The day of the exam (or launch, or performance) is not the time to "hope it works." It's time to deliver. Real success is built on preparation, strategy, and presence.

🛠 Try This in Your Life

📘 Mini Project: Turn Your Next Big Goal into a Study Plan

Think of something you want to achieve that currently feels big, scary, or vague.
Maybe it's:

- Preparing for a certification or job interview
- Launching a side project
- Learning a new skill
- Writing something meaningful
- Building a healthier habit

Step 1: Define Success Clearly

- What does success *look like*? Be specific (e.g., "Finish course and score 85+ on final exam").

Step 2: Break It Down

- List all the components. Use a WBS-like structure. What are the core topics, sub-tasks, or steps involved?

Step 3: Timebox It

- Assign realistic time blocks to each task. Be honest about your capacity. Build in buffer days.

Step 4: Create Weekly Sprints

- Group tasks into weekly chunks. Leave one day for review, one for catch-up or rest.

Step 5: Build a Progress Tracker

- Use a simple spreadsheet, journal, or whiteboard. Track your progress and how you feel along the way. Celebrate the milestones, big or small.

Step 6: Simulate the Real Thing

- Do a trial run under real conditions: a timed mock interview, a presentation test run, or a mini launch to a friend.

🎯 Final Thought

The university entrance exam didn't just get me into a school.

It taught me to lead my life like a project, with structure, consistency, and a mindset of progress over panic.

For anyone wondering how it all ended,
I ranked **2800th out of nearly 3 million participants** nationwide.

That result earned me a place at one of the most reputable state universities in Istanbul:
Yıldız Technical University, in the **Electronics and Communication Engineering Department**, where I entered as the **3rd highest-ranking student** out of a **100-student quota**.

It wasn't luck. It wasn't a miracle.
It was project thinking.
It was showing up every single day, even when I didn't feel like it.
It was trusting the process I built, brick by brick.

Whether you're preparing for your own "exam moment" or facing a completely different kind of challenge, the truth is the same:

You don't rise to the level of your goals. You fall to the level of your systems.
Build better systems. The results will follow.

Bonus Tool: Study Sprint Planner

One of the best decisions I made during my exam prep journey was to structure my study rhythm into **weekly sprints**, short, focused intervals with clear goals, checkpoints, and adjustments. This not only made the workload feel more manageable, but it gave me a real sense of progress, even on tough days.

To help you apply the same method, here's a simple **Study Sprint Planner** you can fill in and reuse each week.

Week	Focus Subjects	Key Topics to Cover	Study Time Goals (hrs)	Mock Exam Score (%)	Confidence Level (1-5)	Reflections & Adjustments
Week 1						
Week 2						
Week 3						
Week 4						
Week 5						
Week 6						

How to Use This Planner

Each row represents one study week. At the start of the week, set your focus, then reflect at the end. Here's what to fill in:

Column	What to Write
Week	Just track which week it is (e.g., Week 1, Week 2...)
Focus Subjects	List 1–2 subjects you'll prioritize that week
Key Topics to Cover	Break those subjects into chapters or topics (e.g., "Ohm's Law, Circuit Diagrams")
Study Time Goals (hrs)	Estimate how many total hours you aim to spend that week
Mock Exam Score (%)	If you do a mock exam, note your score for tracking improvement
Confidence Level (1–5)	Rate how confident you feel (helps you spot emotional highs/lows)
Reflections & Adjustments	End-of-week notes, what worked, what didn't, and what to change next week

Pro Tip:

Don't aim for perfection, aim for momentum. Fill this out at the start of each week and revisit it at the end like a mini project retrospective. You'll be amazed at how clarity builds confidence.

CHAPTER 05

Career Transition to Project Management: From Network Engineer to Finding My Real Path

"Don't be afraid to give up the good to go for the great."
—John D. Rockefeller

5.1. The Comfortable Job That Didn't Fit

When I landed my first job as a **Network Engineer**, I felt like I had made it.

Fresh out of university. Solid diploma in **Electronics and Communication Engineering** from Yıldız Technical University. A reputable company. A real salary. I had the badge, the title, the access card... and, for a while, the pride.

I remember thinking, *"This is what success is supposed to feel like."*

But there was a quiet, creeping thought that began to whisper, not right away, but slowly, steadily:

"Is this it?"

And not in the dramatic, post-college life crisis kind of way.
It was subtler. Like wearing a suit that looked good on paper but felt slightly tight on the shoulders.
Not painful. Just... off.

It Was a Great Job, Just Not *My* Job

Let me be very clear: this wasn't a horror story.
There was no evil boss, no toxic culture, no red flags screaming "Run!"

I was working with good people, solving real problems, configuring switches and routers, getting certified, drawing network diagrams that looked like caffeinated spider webs.

The job was technically challenging, stable, and full of learning opportunities.

And yet...

Every time I completed a task, I felt this weird sense of detachment.
I wasn't lit up.
I wasn't curious to dig deeper.
And over time, the learning curve began to flatten, and so did my energy.

That's when I started asking myself one of the most important questions of my career:

"Just because I'm *good* at this, does that mean I'm *meant* for it?"

Spoiler alert: The answer was no.

What I Loved... and What I Didn't

To understand what came next, I had to get honest with myself about what I actually enjoyed.

Here's what I loved:

- Planning out the delivery timelines for infrastructure projects

- Coordinating with other teams to minimize disruption
- Writing documentation that made sense to non-technical people.
- Presenting complex technical setups in clear terms
- Creating a smooth experience for others

Here's what I didn't:

- Debugging network problems for 3 hours
- Being on-call for midnight outages
- Staring at blinking lights on switches and pretending to feel a deep connection
- Feeling like the work lived in machines more than in people.

I realized that I was more excited about the **execution of projects** than the **technical depth of engineering**.

I wasn't the guy who wanted to go ten layers deep into a command-line rabbit hole.

I was the one asking:

- *When will this go live?*
- *Who's blocked?*
- *What's the risk?*
- *How can we improve this process?*

That's when the fog began to clear.

The Inner Shift

At this point, I had no formal training in project management.
No PMI badge. No agile frameworks.
But I *was* managing workstreams. Planning timelines. Facilitating handovers. Capturing lessons learned.

More importantly, I was **curious** about the people, the process, and the progress.
Not just the packet loss and IP tables.

I was, unknowingly, already wearing the **project manager's hat**, even if my title still said "Engineer."

And when I began researching project management as a real discipline, something lit up in me. It was like someone had just handed me a map with all the street names I had been walking for years, but never knew how to label.

I wasn't broken.
I wasn't unfocused.
I was just on the wrong side of the same room.

5.2. Mapping the Pivot: From Technical Role to Project Manager

Career change doesn't start with a job application.
It starts in your head, and even more so, in your gut.

By year three or four of my life as a Network Engineer, I had developed what I can only describe as *career restlessness*.
It wasn't burnout. It wasn't boredom.
It was the creeping realization I was climbing the wrong ladder, **one leaning against the wrong wall.**

I still showed up, did my work, and delivered quality. But something had shifted.

Instead of asking *"How can I do this better?"* I was asking, *"How much longer do I have to do this?"*

That's when I decided to treat this situation the way I'd treat a troubled project: **pause, assess, and re-scope.**

📌 Step 1: Conducting a Personal Retrospective

Project management has a beautiful ritual: the **retrospective**. It asks three questions after each sprint or phase:

- What went well?
- What didn't go well?
- What should we change?

So, I ran one on my career.

✅ **What went well:**

- Learned how to work under pressure.
- Built strong technical foundations.
- Communicated effectively across departments.
- Gained confidence presenting to different stakeholders.

❌ **What didn't go well:**

- Felt disconnected from the *why* behind my work.
- Spent too much time on tasks that didn't energize me.
- Had no clear development path that aligned with my interests.
- Began avoiding the deep technical work rather than leaning into it.

🔁 **What needed to change:**

- My role had to involve people, planning, strategy, and progress.
- I wanted ownership, not just over tasks, but outcomes.
- I wanted to work *with* people, not just *around* them.

That clarity was liberating; it turned vague dissatisfaction into a roadmap for action.

🗺️ Step 2: Researching the New Terrain

Once I admitted I was ready for a change, I treated it like a project:

- I researched what project managers actually do (beyond the stereotypes)
- I connected with a few who worked in my company's Project Management Office
- I started reading about Waterfall, Agile, Gantt charts, and critical paths (and realized I'd been doing half these things already, just without the jargon)

I was surprised by how **natural** it felt.
Not easy. Not automatic.
But natural.

I wasn't looking for a complete reboot, I was looking for an **evolution**.

The question wasn't "What am I leaving behind?"

It was "What parts of my current role can I carry forward and build on?"

🛠 Step 3: Building a Transition Plan

Once the goal was clear, I built a roadmap.
(Yes, I literally made a roadmap. I couldn't help myself.)

Phase	Focus
Assess	Run a personal retrospective. Identify passion and skill misalignments.
Explore	Research PM roles. Talk to people in the field. Clarify the career shift.
Upskill	Take foundational PM courses. Learn terminology and methodologies.
Shadow	Volunteer to support internal projects or help PMs in small ways.
Apply	Start looking for roles or internal transfers into project coordination.

I wasn't in a rush. I wasn't throwing my old job out the window.
I was just **pivoting intentionally**, step by step.

🧠 What Helped Most

- I treated the transition like a **low-risk internal pilot**, not a leap into the unknown.
- I communicated transparently with my manager about wanting to grow into new responsibilities.
- I said yes to every stretch task involving coordination, communication, or planning, even when it wasn't in my official scope.
- I journaled. A lot. Because clarity lives in reflection.

And eventually, the pieces started aligning.
Opportunities opened in different companies.
People started seeing me *not just as the guy who configures routers*, but as someone who could *lead others through complexity*.

That shift in perception wasn't about my title; it was about how I showed up.

5.3. Translating Tech Skills into PM Strengths

Here's a common misunderstanding when pivoting careers:

You're not starting from scratch. You're starting from experience, just in a new language.

When I landed my first official role as a **Project Manager**, I didn't suddenly erase four years of being a Network Engineer.
I brought it with me, as well as every ticket, outage call, network redesign, server migration, and late-night troubleshooting session.

The only thing that changed was the perspective.

Now, instead of implementing the fix, I was aligning it with strategy, ensuring it fit the timeline, and translating it into business language people could understand.

And that's where my past became my superpower.

What I Brought from My Engineering Life

I may not have known the PMBOK or Prince2 by heart or lived in a world of burndown charts and RAID logs yet...
But I already had **battle-tested instincts** in a few critical areas:

1. Technical fluency

I could speak the language of software developers, engineers, and solution architects.
I didn't have to guess what a firewall migration entailed or why a script might fail.
This helped me earn the team's **trust quickly**, because they knew I understood what they were really dealing with.

2. Root-cause thinking

Engineering taught me that surface-level issues are rarely the real problem.
As a PM, this helped me ask better questions and spot **dependencies** and **risks** early.

3. Explaining complexity simply

As a Network Engineer, I often had to explain weird problems to non-technical stakeholders.
That became a golden PM skill, **translating tech into outcomes.**

4. Calm during chaos!

Nothing teaches you to stay calm under pressure like being on-call at 2 a.m. when a router crashes and half of the customers can't connect to the internet. That **steady hand** became crucial when managing escalations, issues, or difficult clients.

5. Cross-functional collaboration

Even in my old role, I was constantly coordinating with helpdesk teams, security leads, vendors, and operations.
I already knew how to **build alignment without formal authority**, which is almost 80% of project management anyway.

Turning My Experience into Confidence

At first, I had some classic imposter syndrome.

I remember thinking,

"Can I really do this? What if I mess up the planning? What if I miss a dependency?"

But then I remembered the network migration project I led as an engineer and how I:

- Created the step-by-step rollout plan.
- Documented the rollback scenarios.
- Coordinated with five different teams.
- Reported status updates.
- And celebrated the success with zero downtime.

In that moment, I realized:

I'd been managing projects long before I had the title.

That mindset shift changed everything.

🧠 The Real Project Management Isn't in the Tools

People think project management is about tools, such as MS Project, Jira, Smartsheet, and Gantt charts.

Sure, tools help. But they don't make you a PM.

What makes you a PM is:

- Owning outcomes
- Managing uncertainty
- Guiding people through chaos
- Creating plans that flex without breaking.
- Communicating clearly under pressure
- Seeing both the big picture *and* the next step

And guess what?

Most good engineers do this already.
They just call it something else.

5.4. Key Takeaways & Try This in Your Life

Changing careers, especially from something stable and respected, can feel like jumping off a moving train.

There's doubt. There's fear. There's a little voice whispering, *"What if this is a mistake?"*

But here's what I learned by transitioning from Network Engineer to Project Manager:

You don't lose your experience. You repurpose it.
You don't erase your past; you *build on it.*

And if the new path lights you up in a way the old one didn't?
That's not recklessness.
That's clarity. That's alignment.

✅ Key Takeaways

1. Listen to the Discomfort

If your energy dips and curiosity fades, pay attention. Discomfort isn't always a red flag; it might be a signal that growth is calling you somewhere else.

2. Run a Personal Retrospective

Look back on your work. What do you enjoy? What drains you? What moments felt meaningful? These are clues for your next step.

3. Treat Your Transition Like a Project

Build a roadmap: Assess → Explore → Upskill → Shadow → Apply. Each phase gives you more clarity and reduces fear of the unknown.

4. You're Not Starting from Zero

Spot the skills you already use, like communication, problem-solving, and stakeholder management. They're often hiding in plain sight.

5. The Title Doesn't Make the Leader

You don't need permission to think like a Project Manager. Start leading where you are. Influence without authority. Deliver outcomes. The title will catch up.

🛠 Try This in Your Life

📋 Mini Project: Career Pivot Reflection Map

Block 30 minutes this week to run your own career retrospective and create a roadmap. Grab a notebook or a digital doc and fill this out:

🧠 Self-Retrospective

Question	Your Reflection
What tasks energize you?	
What tasks drain you?	
When do you feel most proud of your work?	
What roles or responsibilities do you admire in others?	

Transition Roadmap

Phase	Actions
Explore	Research 2–3 roles that intrigue you
Upskill	Find one course or mentor conversation you can do this month.
Translate	List five skills from your current job that you can carry forward.
Test	Volunteer for a new task, project, or cross-functional opportunity
Reflect	After 1–2 months, assess: Do you feel more aligned?

This isn't about quitting your job tomorrow.
It's about *getting intentional*, so you don't spend 10 years on autopilot.

Your next role isn't just about what's available.
It's about who you're becoming.

CHAPTER 06

The Wedding Project: Planning Love Like a Product Launch

"A successful marriage requires falling in love many times, always with the same person."
—Mignon McLaughlin

6.1. The Most Beautiful Chaos I Ever Managed

People say weddings are the happiest day of your life.
Whoever said that clearly never had to organize one.

Don't get me wrong, our wedding was beautiful.
It was joyful, emotional, and filled with moments I'll never forget.
But behind every magical photo and heartfelt vow was a high-stakes, multi-stakeholder, time-boxed, emotionally charged, scope-creeping, budget-sensitive project...also known as **"getting married."**

And of course, because I had already started thinking in project management mode, I didn't just plan a wedding.

I **led** it, like a mission-critical go-live... with flowers.

💍 Love Meets Logistics

When my now-wife and I decided to get married, we knew two things:

1. We wanted it to be meaningful, intimate, and representative of who we were.
2. We had **zero idea** how to plan a wedding.

Cue the spiral: venues, vendors, dates, guest lists, seating charts, dress codes, menu tastings, traditions (and which ones to skip) ... and opinions. So Many Opinions.

That's when I realized: **this is just another project.**

- The deliverable? A wedding day we'd actually enjoy.
- The timeline? Immovable.
- The risks? Too many to count.
- The client? My wife (make no mistake, I was not the sponsor here).
- The team? Us. And a whole bunch of volunteers with strong opinions and questionable availability.
- The success criteria? We both said, "I do", and still liked each other at the end of it.

🎯 Fixed Deadline. Emotional Stakeholders. Moving Targets.

What makes weddings uniquely difficult to manage isn't the scale; it's the **combination of emotion and expectation**.

You're not just managing tasks. You're managing:

- Parents' dreams
- Guests' logistics
- Cultural or religious expectations
- Personal desires
- And each other's stress levels

And because it's your wedding, everyone feels like they have a **stake in it**.

People who hadn't messaged me in a year were suddenly experts in table layout.
Aunties asked about invitations before we'd picked a date.
Vendors ghosted us.
Some friends couldn't attend. Others showed up with plus ones we didn't know about.

It was my first time managing a project where the stakeholders treated scope like a buffet table.

Why I Chose to Lead It Like a Project

Here's what I knew: we had one shot.
There was no "hotfix" for a wedding that goes off the rails.

And I didn't want to look back and think:

- "We should've budgeted better."
- "I wish we'd planned for bad weather."
- "Why didn't we just outsource the seating chart?"

So, I treated it like any other critical project in my life:

1. **Create a high-level plan with clear milestones.**
2. **Define roles and responsibilities (me vs. her vs. family)**
3. **Identify high-risk elements early (venue, weather, budget, vendors)**
4. **Communicate constantly and clearly.**
5. **Track progress without turning it into a second full-time job.**

And you know what? It worked.
Not perfectly. **But beautifully enough**.
We all know project management isn't about rigidity, and it's about calm structure inside emotional chaos.

And weddings are just like that, **emotional environments with countdown clocks.**

6.2. Creating the Wedding Work Breakdown Structure (WBS)

At a certain point in the planning process, probably somewhere between venue-hunting and tasting cake samples, I realized the only way to survive without losing our minds or our relationship was to stop thinking like a groom...

...and start thinking like a **PM on a deadline.**

I opened my laptop. Created a new file. Named it: **"Wedding WBS – Do or Die Edition."**

And I started breaking the beast down.

Step 1: From Giant Mess to Manageable Pieces

Project managers use something called a **Work Breakdown Structure (WBS)** to simplify complexity.
The idea is simple: break down a giant deliverable (like "Plan Wedding") into smaller, actionable components.

And that's exactly what we did.

We categorized everything into core areas:

1. **Venue & Logistics**
2. **Guest Experience**
3. **Ceremony & Program Flow**
4. **Food & Drinks**
5. **Design & Decor**
6. **Wardrobe & Styling**
7. **Vendors & Contracts**
8. **Contingency Planning**

Each of those had its own sub-items. For example:

- **Venue & Logistics**
    - Shortlist venues
    - Visit the top 3.
    - Book venue & pay deposit.

- Arrange guest transportation.
- Coordinate with the venue manager.

- **Guest Experience**
  - Final guest list.
  - Save-the-dates.
  - Formal invitations.
  - RSVP tracking.
  - Seating chart.
  - Gifts & thank you notes.

- **Ceremony & Program Flow**
  - Vows
  - Music selections
  - Master of Ceremonies briefing
  - Timeline of the day
  - Cue cards and handoffs.

I can't tell you how much relief this brought.
Suddenly, it wasn't "We have a million things to do."
It became, "Today, we finalize the seating chart and confirm the photographer."

Clarity. Focus. Progress.

🎯 Step 2: Assigning Ownership

Once the WBS was in place, we did something most couples skip: **we assigned roles**.

Not just "You take this, I take that," but clear **ownership**.

- I handled all vendor communication (emails, calls, payment timelines)
- My wife took the lead on styling and guest experience.
- We reviewed financials together every two weeks.
- One very organized friend became our unofficial "wedding day coordinator."
- Another close friend took charge of capturing behind-the-scenes photos.

This wasn't about being rigid; it was about removing ambiguity.
Because *"We'll do it together"* sounds romantic... until both people assume the other is handling it.

🛠 The Planning Tool Stack

No fancy software. We used:

- **Google Sheets** – for budgets, checklists, and guest lists
- **Google Drive** – for contracts, vendor info, reference photos
- **A simple Kanban board** – for tasks and visual progress (dragging a task to "done" = best feeling ever)
- **WhatsApp group** – for quick updates with our small planning crew

It wasn't corporate. It wasn't polished.
But it was ours. And it worked.

💡 The WBS Was More Than a Tool

It wasn't just about staying on track.
The WBS became a **communication tool**, a **stress reducer**, and a **relationship saver**.

Any time things started to feel overwhelming, we didn't panic; we just opened the sheet, picked a manageable task, and kept going.

We weren't just planning a wedding.
We were delivering a mission with heart.

6.3. Budget Battles and Vendor Diplomacy

If the WBS gave us structure, the budget snapped us back to reality.

Because love may be priceless...
...but everything else has **a line item, an invoice, and a deadline.**

And let me tell you: nothing tests your conflict resolution skills quite like sitting down with your partner to discuss **why decoration costs almost as much as your first car.**

The Budget vs. The Dream

At first, we had no clear number in mind.
We just wanted something "beautiful, but not over the top."
(Yes, I can hear your knowing smile through the screen.)

But when the quotes started rolling in, we realized that "not over the top" was a relative term especially when vendors hear the word *wedding.*

The venue wanted one deposit.
The caterer needed another.
The florist charged more because it was peak season.
The photographer's "premium package" made it feel like we were producing a Hollywood blockbuster.

So, we did what every good PM does when faced with financial ambiguity:

We built a budget tracker and locked in the scope.

Building Our Wedding Budget Tracker

We started a shared Google Sheet and created three columns:

1. **Estimated Cost**
2. **Quoted Cost**
3. **Actual Cost**

And we categorized it all:

Category	Est. Cost	Quoted	Actual	Notes
Venue & Catering	€X	€Y	€Z	50% deposit paid
Photography & Video	€	€	€	Negotiated for digital-only
Music & Entertainment	€	€	€	DJ instead of a live band
Flowers & Decor	€	€	€	Downscaled centerpiece design
Wedding Attire	€	€	€	Tailoring included
Gifts & Stationery	€	€	€	Opted for digital invites

The result?
We had a **clear view** of where money was going and where we needed to adjust.

More importantly, it turned emotionally loaded conversations into data-driven decisions.
This wasn't "you're spending too much on flowers."
It was "we're €500 over in decor, can we pull that from another category?"

Vendor Management 101: The Diplomacy Game

Working with vendors was... enlightening.

Some were lovely, responsive, creative, and flexible.
Others disappeared for a week and returned like nothing happened.
Some tacked-on hidden costs.
Others required repeated follow-up to confirm the simplest details.

It felt like managing third-party suppliers in a software project:

- Different timelines
- Varying definitions of "urgent"
- Lots of enthusiasm up front, followed by gradual ghosting.

That's when I applied a classic PM trick:

Create a Vendor Log with contact info, deadlines, payment status, and confirmed scope.

Every vendor got a slot. Every meeting had minutes. Every payment had a trail.

I became politely assertive, a skill every project manager needs.

- "Thanks for your quote, can you confirm if setup is included?"
- "Just looping back to our last conversation, can you share the updated version by Friday?"
- "Before we sign, can we clarify the cancellation terms in writing?"

Not aggressive. Just professional.
Because a wedding may be emotional, but the execution should be **structured.**

🔍 Scope Creep, but Make It Personal

The toughest part?
Saying no to "just one more thing."

A friend would suggest an extra decorative touch.
A parent would ask for a traditional element.
Pinterest (that charming saboteur) would show us "must-have" ideas... daily.

But just like in project delivery, we had to protect the scope:

- "That's beautiful, but doesn't fit our theme."
- "We love that idea, but it's not in the budget."

"Let's save that for the anniversary party." 😅

💡 What We Learned

- **Transparency diffuses tension** – When you're honest about costs and priorities, you avoid resentment.
- **Vendors are partners, not magicians** – They'll do great work if you manage them like collaborators, not wish-granters.
- **Trade-offs are inevitable** – The sooner you accept that, the more peaceful the planning becomes.

And most importantly:

The perfect wedding isn't the one with the biggest budget.
It's the one where the people feel most loved, and the couple feels most at ease.

6.4. The Wedding Day: Go-Live and Golden Lessons

There's a certain kind of silence on the morning of your wedding.
Not nervous silence.
Not awkward silence.
A kind of **calm-before-the-launch silence**.

We'd done the work.
The vendors were briefed.
The families were aligned (mostly).

The outfits were steamed.
The seating chart was revised more times than the final code commit before going live.

Now... it was go time.

The Final Countdown

Like any go-live, there were butterflies in the stomach.
Except this time, the butterflies were in tuxedos.

We woke up early. Got dressed. Double-checked the emergency bag. Printed out a copy of the event timeline. Gave our "wedding day coordinator" friend a heartfelt briefing that sounded suspiciously like a sprint stand-up.

Everything was ready.

And just like any major go-live, **things started going sideways** immediately.

- A vendor arrived late because of traffic.
- One of the flower arrangements wasn't what we ordered.
- A guest brought an unexpected plus one, creating chaos in the seating plan.
- The AV system briefly glitched right before our walk-in song.
- And someone (who shall remain nameless) forgot to bring the rings to the venue.

But the strangest thing happened...

We didn't panic.

Why Things Didn't Break

We didn't panic because we'd built margin.
We'd rehearsed the ceremony. We'd made backup lists.
And most importantly, we'd **accepted imperfection**.

This wasn't a test of logistics anymore.
This was about presence.

The wedding wasn't following a schedule. It was unfolding in real time.

It reminded me of project go-lives I'd seen in the corporate world:

- You can't control every detail.
- The best preparation creates flexibility, not rigidity.
- What matters most is the outcome and how people feel at the end of the day.

♡ The Outcome That Mattered

At the end of the day:

- We said our vows.
- We laughed and drank a lot.
- We danced until our legs hurt.
- Our guests felt connected, welcomed, and joyful.
- And we felt completely, unapologetically, *married.*

The project didn't go perfectly, but it went beautifully.
Because it was real.
It reflected us, not just in the aesthetic, but in how we managed the chaos.

It wasn't about whether the flower arch was symmetrical.
It was about being present with the people we loved most.

And honestly? That's the definition of project success: human, heartfelt, and real.

PM Lessons from the Aisle

Looking back, I walked away with a few powerful reminders:

- **You can't plan your way out of unpredictability. But you can prepare your way through it.**
- **A calm mindset is more valuable than a perfect schedule.**
- **Every go-live is emotional, whether it's a product launch or saying "I do." The job isn't just execution; it's leadership through emotion.**

6.5. Key Takeaways & Try This in Your Life

Planning a wedding wasn't just a celebration; it was a crash course in real-life project management: high emotion, fixed timelines, unpredictable variables, and the most important stakeholder of all, someone you love.

What made it work wasn't a perfect plan.
It was just enough structure to stay calm, and just enough flexibility to stay human.

✅ Key Takeaways

1. Treat Big Life Moments Like Projects

When emotions run high and everything feels chaotic, add structure. Even a simple WBS or timeline brings clarity and calm.

2. Clear Roles Save Relationships

Avoid assumption-driven chaos. Assign ownership early. Know who's handling what. "We'll do it together" sounds romantic but often leads to confusion.

3. Vendors Are Like External Partners

Set expectations. Document agreements. Communicate clearly. And be kind but assertive, especially when things get off track.

4. Build Margin into the Plan

Something *will* go wrong. What matters is whether you've created buffer time, backup plans, and enough emotional space to stay grounded.

5. Done Is Better Than Perfect, Especially in Love

Not every detail will land. But if you end the day feeling present, joyful, and connected, that's a 100% project success rate in my book.

🛠 Try This in Your Life

💍 Plan a Life Event Using PM Principles

Whether it's a wedding, birthday party, vacation, or even a move, apply a mini project management approach to keep it stress-free and joyful:

Big moments are easier to enjoy when they're planned with intention, not perfection.

Life Event Planning Sheet

Task	Owner	Deadline	Risk	Backup Plan
Choose venue	Me	Jan 10	Overbooked	Call two alternates
Final guest list	Partner	Jan 15	Conflicts	Add buffer chairs and tables
Book caterer	Me	Jan 20	Menu issues	Offer a simple vegetarian backup
Send invites	Partner	Jan 25	RSVP delay	Send one reminder message
Timeline of the day	Me	Jan 28	Overrun	Add 15-minute buffers between segments

---

PM Challenge:

Try managing a non-work life event this way.
Keep it simple. Make it collaborative.
Notice how people respond differently when roles are clear, and emotions aren't running the show.

Final Thought

The wedding wasn't just about flowers, venues, or timelines.

It was about saying:
"We're in this together. Through every moving part. Through every surprise. Through every success and stumble."

And if you can plan a wedding with love, leadership, and laughter?
You can lead just about any project life throws your way.

Bonus Tool: Wedding or Life Event Project Tracker

Whether you're planning a wedding, baby shower, milestone birthday, or any big life moment, this simple tracker keeps tasks visible, deadlines clear, and ownership defined, so you can enjoy the journey without drowning in details.

Pro Tip: Customize it with your event categories and use status updates weekly to stay on track together.

Task	Owner	Due Date	Status	Notes
Book venue	Me	6/1/2025	Not Started	Visit the top 3 options
Finalize the guest list	My wife	6/5/2025	In Progress	Waiting for 5 RSVP responses
Send invites	My wife	6/10/2025	Not Started	
Confirm menu	Me	6/12/2025	Not Started	Check the vegetarian option
Assign a day-of coordinator.	Close Friend	5/15/2025	Completed	Brief them on the timeline

CHAPTER 07

Dubai Relocation: Managing a Life Change Like a Global Rollout

"You can't connect the dots looking forward; you can only connect them looking backward."
—Steve Jobs

7.1. When Life Hands You a One-Way Ticket

Some life decisions are made with spreadsheets.
Others, with gut instinct.
And some... with both open in separate tabs.

The decision to move to **Dubai** was one of those.

We weren't running from something.

We were moving **toward possibility**, a new experience, a new challenge, a new chapter.

And unlike many who relocate with a vague plan or blind faith, I was stepping into something very specific:
A leadership role at a **major international broadcaster** that was ready to reinvent itself.

Their vision?
To transform their entire television and content ecosystem, launch streaming solutions, build web platforms, create mobile apps, and reinvent the digital experience.
And my role was clear: **build and lead the digital project management team** to make it all happen.

They offered a **relocation package**, logistical support, and an opportunity I couldn't ignore.

But the decision to say "yes" still required something deeper than a signature.
It required **courage**.

✈️ A Move That Wasn't Just Professional

At the time, my wife and I were settled in Istanbul.
We had jobs we liked, a rhythm that felt familiar, a community we could rely on.

But deep down, we felt it.

The itch.
The question.
That quiet voice asking:

"What if we just tried something completely different?"

So, when the offer came, it didn't feel random.
It felt like the answer we were already looking for.

We were excited.
We were ready.
At least... that's what we kept telling ourselves.

Welcome to the Master Relocation Plan

We knew moving across the world wasn't just a trip, it was an operation.

And if there's one thing I've learned in life, **if it feels big, treat it like a project.**

So, I did.

I opened a fresh folder on my laptop, titled it "Dubai Move," and inside it went:

- A **Work Breakdown Structure** for every step of the relocation
- A list of critical documents
- A phased budget
- A shared calendar for decision points
- And a personal checklist that mixes both logistics and emotions.

There was no room for winging it, not with international banking, visa hurdles, housing logistics, and life-uprooting timelines hanging in the balance.

The deliverable? Land in Dubai safely, legally, and sanely.
The stakeholder expectation? Begin a new life with as little chaos as possible.

From Local Comfort to Global Complexity

When I arrived in Dubai, suitcase in hand, excitement in my heart, I quickly realized this wasn't just a **relocation**.
It was a **reinvention.**

Until that point, my entire professional life had been in Turkey.
I worked with teams where **99% of the people shared my culture, language, humor, and worldview.**

Now?

I had stepped into an office building with **nearly 100 different nationalities.** A melting pot of accents, expectations, work habits, decision-making styles, and unspoken cultural codes.

It was beautiful... and disorienting.

Simple things like giving feedback, setting a meeting, or even making small talk had to be **relearned.**
Because the way I was used to operating didn't always translate.

And every interaction became an opportunity to **observe, adjust, and adapt.**

And if that wasn't enough of a challenge, I was also doing it **alone**, at least at first.

My wife and I had agreed that I would go ahead and get things set up.
So for the first **three months**, I was navigating this new life solo.

No familiar face to decompress with.
No "how was your day?" over dinner.
Just me, a new job, a new apartment, and the dizzying heat of Dubai.

That period taught me a lot about **resilience**, **cultural intelligence**, and what it really means to lead in an environment where you're not just managing projects... you're **rebuilding your identity.**

🔄 A Project with No UAT Environment

Relocation doesn't come with a user acceptance test.
You don't get a soft launch.
There's no "pilot environment" for living in a new country.

You either go, or you don't.
You adapt, or you struggle.

And while we had a structured plan, I quickly learned that:

- Not all systems work the way they say they will.
- Not everything goes according to schedule.
- And no matter how well you plan, there will always be emotional curveballs.

But we had each other (eventually).
We had the vision.
And most importantly, we had a mindset that saw this not as a leap into the unknown...

...but as a **life project** worth delivering.

7.2. Building the Dubai Relocation Plan Like a Program

You know that feeling when you kick off a massive transformation project, excited at first, until you realize just how many moving parts there are?

That was the Dubai move.

Except this time, I wasn't just managing cross-functional teams.
I was the team.

No project coordinator. No admin. No global PMO.
Just me, a shared Google Drive folder, a mountain of tasks, and a growing realization that **this relocation needed to be treated like a full-on program.**

As always, I did what I do when things get big and fuzzy:
I broke it down.

Phase 1 – Planning: Discovery and Design

Like any good program, I started with **discovery and alignment**.
If I were going to deliver this relocation successfully, I would have to define:

- **Scope:** What exactly are we moving? (Just ourselves? Furniture? Career aspirations? Dreams?)
- **Timeline:** When do I start? When does my wife join? When does "settled" begin?
- **Risks:** What could go wrong logistically, emotionally, and financially?
- **Budget**: What's the realistic cost, and where do we build in contingency?

We created a **relocation charter**, even if unofficial. Something that aligned expectations and kept us grounded when the to-do list got overwhelming.

This wasn't just about moving. It was about building a soft landing for a major life transition.

Phase 2 – Execution: The Migration Begins

Once the framework was set, we moved into **execution**.

This phase included things like:

- **Legal & Admin Setup**
  - Visa applications
  - Residency requirements
  - International health insurance
  - Banking and tax consultations
- **Housing Logistics**
  - Researching rentals remotely
  - Securing temporary housing for phase one
  - Navigating Dubai's tenancy processes (spoiler: not fun)
- **Asset Inventory & Shipping**
  - What should come with me?
  - What should go into storage?
  - What should be sold or donated?
- **Financial Planning**
  - First-month burn rate.
  - Emergency buffer
  - Currency exchange considerations
- **Relationship Management**
  - Informing family and friends
  - Managing emotional expectations
  - Scheduling our "mini goodbyes" with key people

I created a **master relocation tracker** with deadlines, ownership (me vs. wife), and decision status for every task.

It wasn't fancy, but it gave us clarity. And in moments of chaos, clarity is everything.

Phase 3 – Integration: Landing and Settling

This was the trickiest phase because, unlike packing boxes, **emotional adaptation has no checklist**.

Even though I landed with a clear plan, I quickly realized that:

- Culture shock hits you in waves
- Admin tasks take longer than expected (and require more patience than caffeine)
- You start over socially, mentally, and sometimes professionally.

Some days I felt energized and inspired.
Other days, I felt like an outsider with a fancy title and a silent flat.

To cope, I created a mini **post-move stabilization plan**:

- Daily routines for mental structure
- Coffee meetings with colleagues from different cultures (to learn and connect)
- Weekend check-ins with my wife over video (before she moved)
- A personal weekly retro: What went well this week? What felt off? What can I adjust?

This wasn't just "settling in."
This was **self-leadership in a high-change environment**.

🎯 A Program with People at Its Core

Looking back, the success of the Dubai relocation didn't come from how well I filled out forms or how early I booked the flights.

It came from how well I:

- Communicated clearly and often.
- Built routines to create stability.
- Prepared emotionally, not just logistically.
- Treated my *own* well-being as a project milestone.
- Stayed flexible when reality didn't match the plan.

Because no matter how great your roadmap is, the most important resource you manage in any program is **yourself.**

7.3. Leading in a Melting Pot: The Multicultural Project Reality

Nothing, and I literally mean nothing, prepared me for the cultural cocktail that was my new office in Dubai: a vibrant mashup of accents, mindsets, and unspoken rules.

One moment, I was in a stand-up with colleagues from India, Lebanon, and Syria.

Next, I was reviewing requirements with a product owner from the UK, a UX designer from Egypt, and a tech lead from the Netherlands.

And all of this was happening in a language that wasn't native to **any** of us.

Welcome to the **United Nations of project delivery.**

It was dynamic. Inspiring.
And, at times, completely overwhelming.

🌐 Same Words, Different Worlds

One of the first things I learned was that **language fluency ≠ meaning fluency**.

Take a phrase as simple as "Let's align."
For some, that meant a formal sync-up with slides and action items.
For others, it meant a quick chat over coffee.
And for a few, it meant nodding politely... and then doing exactly what they were going to do anyway. 😅

So, I had to recalibrate.
I couldn't assume anything.
I had to **observe, ask, and adapt.**

This was no longer about just delivering a project; it was about **learning how to lead people who play by different rules.**

🧭 Culture Isn't Just Flags and Food

It's about the deeper operating system behind how people work:

- **How people give feedback** (direct vs. indirect)
- **How they view time** (flexible vs. fixed)
- **How decisions get made** (individual vs. consensus)
- **How status is expressed** (title, age, relationship, experience)
- **How silence is interpreted** (comfort vs. tension)

I had to unlearn habits I didn't even know were cultural.

In Turkey, for example, long pauses in meetings might mean someone is disengaged.
In Japan, it could mean they're thinking deeply.
In the UK, disagreement is often wrapped in politeness.
In the Netherlands, it hits you straight like a bullet train.

Every 1:1, every team check-in became a chance to **decode the invisible project layer: culture.**

🤝 From Team Building to Trust Building

I quickly realized that my effectiveness as a leader wouldn't depend on certifications or Gantt charts.

It would be about **trust.**

And trust looks different across cultures.

Here's what worked:

- **Weekly 1:1s**, not just for status updates, but for understanding people's lives, goals, and frustrations.
- **Cultural curiosity**, I'd ask team members to teach me one thing about their home country over coffee.
- **Transparent priorities**, I made it clear what was flexible and what wasn't, so expectations were aligned.
- **Celebrating small wins**, especially when language or distance makes people feel disconnected.

And I had to **model vulnerability,** too.

I shared how weird it felt to lead in a new environment.
How I missed home.
How I was learning alongside them.
And that made people open up in ways that created real cohesion.

📈 The Unexpected PM Lessons

This multicultural project environment taught me more than any certification ever could:

- **Assume nothing. Ask everything.**
- **Be clear, then be clearer.**
- **Make room for every voice, especially the quiet ones.**
- **Create shared definitions of success, don't assume your "done" is their "done."**
- **And when in doubt: listen more, lead softer.**

Because no project can thrive without psychological safety.
And in multicultural teams, that safety isn't granted. It's earned, one conversation at a time.

7.4. Key Takeaways & Try This in Your Life

Relocating to Dubai wasn't just a change of address; it was a transformation project with no rollback option.
Leading a multicultural team wasn't just a job; it was a crash course in human-centered leadership.

I came in thinking I'd be running programs.
I left realizing I'd been rewriting my own operating system.

✅ Key Takeaways

1. Treat Major Life Changes Like Programs

Break them into phases. Create structure. Track progress. But also bake in buffer time, mental space, and emotional checkpoints.

2. Adaptability Is the New PM Superpower

It's not just about managing tasks, it's about reading the room, adjusting your style, and staying grounded when everything around you feels foreign.

3. Culture Is the Invisible Backlog

You won't see it in Jira, but it shapes how everything gets built, communicated, and delivered. The more you understand it, the better you lead.

4. People Need More Than Clarity, They Need Safety

In diverse teams, trust is currency. Invest early. Be real. And don't just celebrate deliverables, celebrate connection.

5. Leadership Is Learned in the Gray Areas

Certifications teach you frameworks. Real life teaches you how to listen across cultures, lead through ambiguity, and grow when the ground shifts beneath you.

🛠 Try This in Your Life

🌍 Mini Project: Relocate Your Mindset

You don't have to move countries to experience transformation.
Try managing your next big "life pivot" as if it were a global transformation program:

Relocation Thinking Template

Step	Action	Example
Define Scope	What are you changing? What stays?	Changing jobs, staying in the same city
Identify Stakeholders	Who's affected by this change?	Partner, kids, boss, clients
Break It Down	What phases does this move have?	Notice period, job onboarding, and rework the daily routine
Cultural Awareness	What's different in this new environment?	Startup pace vs. corporate structure
Build Integration Routines	What new habits will help you adapt?	Daily journaling, team lunch once a week, monthly retrospectives
Define Success	What will "settled" look and feel like?	Feeling confident, regaining structure, rebuilding social circle

💡 *Pro Tip:* The next time you feel out of place or overwhelmed in a new situation, don't ask "Why is this so hard?"
Instead ask:

"What would a great project manager do in this moment?"

Because chances are… they'd listen, plan, adapt, and lead with empathy.
So can you.

CHAPTER 08

The PhD Project: The Research That Almost Broke Me (and What Saved Me)

"Education is not the learning of facts, but the training of the mind to think."
—Albert Einstein

8.1. A PhD in Determination

Some people climb mountains.
Some run marathons.
I chose to write a PhD thesis while working full-time, leading complex digital transformation programs, trying not to lose my mind in the process.

And if I'm being honest, it wasn't one of those "I always dreamed of getting a PhD" moments.

It was more like:

"I'm passionate about leadership. I want to explore it deeply. And if I don't do this now, I may never get the chance."

So, I committed, fully aware that it wouldn't be easy.

But I also knew one thing very clearly: **I needed flexibility.**

My MBA at the University of London had been incredible, stretching, challenging, and rewarding. But flying back and forth between Dubai and the UK for classes and exams while juggling a demanding role?

That was rough.

I didn't want that again.

That's why I took a different route.

🎓 Choosing My Own Path (and My Own Pain)

I enrolled at **Istanbul Okan University**, a newer, forward-thinking school that offered exactly what I needed:

- A strong academic structure
- A faculty open to new leadership topics.
- And most importantly, **flexibility** in class attendance and research timelines

It wasn't the most prestigious name.
But it was the right fit, a key lesson for anyone pursuing education later in life: choose what matches your life, not just your ego.

And once I got in, I knew exactly what I wanted to explore.

🧭 Research from the Front Lines

By this point, I had led teams in Turkey, Dubai, and across global offices. I'd seen firsthand how different leadership styles shaped project results, not just the metrics, but the mood, the morale, and the magic that makes teams go the extra mile.

So, I thought, *why not study this properly?*

My thesis became a natural extension of my real-world experience:

"The Impact of Servant and Inclusive Leadership on Project Success in Multicultural Organizations"

This wasn't just theory, it was the stuff I was living every day.
From the way I ran meetings, to how I resolved conflicts, to the culture I tried to build as a leader, **this research felt personal.**

And that's what made it powerful and profoundly exhausting.

⏳ The Start Was Slow, But the Spiral Was Fast

Like many PhD students, I started strong.
I had folders. Literature reviews. A research framework.
I even created a Trello board labelled: "PhD Master Plan – 3-Year Journey."

Year 1 went well enough. I attended the necessary classes, drafted proposals, and started reading like a man possessed.
I felt like a proper scholar, with highlighters, margin notes, and the whole academic vibe.

But by Year 2?

Life. Happened.

Big work projects.
Family needs.
Leadership pressure.
Burnout cycles.

And the PhD folder?
It just... sat there. Staring at me. Whispering guilt.

Some weeks, I couldn't bring myself to open a single article.
Other weeks, I'd make up for it by binge-writing 3,000 words like I was chasing a publishing deadline.

And through it all, I kept asking:

"Why am I doing this again?"

The Answer Wasn't in the Thesis, It Was in the Transformation

I wasn't doing this to get called "Dr. Ozgur."
I wasn't doing it to impress people on LinkedIn.

I was doing it because I wanted to **become the kind of leader who doesn't just manage people but understands them. Supports them. Helps them.** Especially when they come from different cultures, speak different first languages, or see the world through a different lens.

And that's what kept me going.

Even when I was writing surveys late at night.
Even when my supervisor sent back a draft with more red than black.
Even when I thought about quitting.

Because this was more than a degree.

It was a **project of persistence**, powered by purpose.

8.2. Structuring the Research Like a Real Project

One reason PhDs often drag, or get abandoned entirely, is because they're massive, vague, and emotionally draining.

There's no client breathing down your neck.
No real deadlines (at least not ones that feel real).
And no project sponsor to escalate delays to, unless you count your inner critic, who is notoriously unhelpful.

Which meant the only way I could survive this was by doing what I knew best:
Managing my thesis like a project.

Actually... like a **program**.

Because it wasn't one deliverable.
It was a complex series of interconnected workstreams: literature review, methodology, data collection, analysis, writing, rewriting, citations, formatting... and oh yeah, defending it all in front of a committee.

Step 1: Define Scope, Time, and Quality

I started by treating it like a proper project kickoff.

Project Element	Definition
Scope	Complete a PhD thesis on leadership styles and their influence on project success in multicultural organizations
Timeline	~3 years (with clear milestones)
Success Criteria	Thesis approved, defense passed, publication-ready format.
Stakeholders	Myself, thesis advisor, committee members, and the academic board
Risks	Burnout, work-life imbalance, scope creep, and access issues during data collection
Assumptions	Access to diverse multicultural project managers for surveys/interviews

This sounds basic, but writing it out helped me treat this as **a real commitment**, not just an intellectual hobby.

Step 2: Build a Research WBS (Work Breakdown Structure)

Here's how I broke it down:

1. **Initiation**
    - Research topic selection.
    - Supervisor assignment.
    - Initial proposal and concept approval.
2. **Planning**
    - Literature review matrix.
    - Conceptual framework drafting.
    - Research questions and hypothesis formulation.
3. **Execution – Phase 1**
    - Designing survey tools
    - Ethics approval
    - Pilot testing

4. **Execution – Phase 2**
    - Full-scale data collection
    - Statistical analysis (SPSS quickly became my new frenemy)
    - Interview coding and synthesis.
5. **Closure**
    - Drafting each chapter
    - Editing and revisions
    - Supervisor review cycles
    - Final submission and viva preparation

Breaking it into phases and tasks gave me control over something that usually feels infinite.

⏱ Step 3: Use Sprints and Milestones

I treated each research task like a **4-week sprint**.

Examples:

- Sprint 1: Read 10 articles and write the Literature Review intro.
- Sprint 2: Submit survey to 50 project managers and clean data.
- Sprint 3: Write the methodology section and get supervisor feedback.

And I celebrated small wins.
Even finishing a section of Chapter 2 felt like shipping a release.

📊 Step 4: Track Progress Visually

I created a ridiculously simple tool that saved my sanity:

- A progress dashboard in Google Sheets
- Columns for each section of the thesis
- Status tags: **Not Started**, **In Progress**, **Rework Needed**, **Submitted**, **Approved**

Color-coded, of course.
And every time I turned a cell from red to green, it felt like winning the Olympics.

What Didn't Work

Let's be real, it wasn't all clean and perfect.

- I over planned the early stages and underestimated the emotional fatigue.
- Sometimes I used "planning" as procrastination.
- I underestimated how much mental space I'd need during work deadlines.
- And yes, I absolutely ignored my own tracker for two months straight at one point.

But you know what?

Even though the plan wasn't perfect, the **mindset** kept me going.

Because project thinking isn't just about Gantt charts, **it's about creating momentum when motivation fades.**

8.3. Lessons from Leadership: What My Thesis Taught Me About Real Teams

If you asked me before I started my PhD what I thought I'd discover, I would've confidently said this:

"Servant leadership and inclusive leadership improve project success under all circumstances. That's a given."

It was logical. It aligned with global research. It matched my own leadership values.
And frankly, it's what most of the literature has already said.

But then I did the research.

I collected data from **over 300 white-collar project professionals in Dubai**, one of the world's most multicultural work environments. I ran **structural equation modeling**. I cross-checked dimensions, impact factors, and outcomes.

And the results?

They surprised me. Actually... they shocked me.

The Aha Moment: Not All Leadership Works Everywhere

Contrary to most global studies, especially those conducted in more **monocultural environments**, my research found that:

- **Servant leadership behaviors** had **minimal or no consistent positive correlation** with project success in multicultural teams in Dubai.
- Similarly, a leader's **support for diversity and inclusion** did **not consistently improve project outcomes**.
- In fact, **some dimensions** (like "encouragement" and "participation support") even had a **negative effect** in certain cases.

Let that land.

The leadership approach praised for being empathetic, fair, and empowering **didn't consistently drive success** in a highly diverse, high-stakes project environment like Dubai.

Why? Because **context matters. Culture matters. And because leadership is never one-size-fits-all.**

Breaking It Down: The Real Data

My study broke leadership down into measurable behaviors across eight servant leadership dimensions (empowerment, accountability, tolerance, humbleness, etc.) and measured their impact on two key outcomes:

1. **Project Execution Success**
2. **Project Planning Success**

Here's what the data showed:

- **Encouragement**, often seen as a positive trait, actually had a **negative effect** on both execution and planning success.
- **Administrative management behaviors** had a **positive impact**, suggesting that structure and clarity were more effective than soft support.
- The **support for diversity participation**, expected to enhance inclusion, **negatively correlated** with execution success.

The Bigger Insight: Situational Leadership Is Essential

This wasn't just a plot twist in my thesis; it was a wake-up call for my leadership style.

It told me:

- That cultural complexity can completely rewrite what works.
- That **servant leadership**, while noble, may be **misread in some environments** as indecisive or weak.
- That **over-encouraging participation** can sometimes create confusion or reduce efficiency when cultural norms favor authority and structure.

And most of all:

That great leadership isn't about **being nice**.
It's about being effective, for that team, in that moment, within that context.

The Dubai Lesson for Global Leaders

If you're leading in a multicultural environment, and especially on global project teams, here's what my research suggests:

- Don't default to any single leadership style, no matter how trendy or evidence-backed it is.
- **Read the room, and the room might have 15 cultural operating systems.**
- Sometimes, teams need clarity more than collaboration.
- Sometimes, structure trumps flexibility.
- And often, the best leadership is the one that flexes, **not the one that flatters.**

What Changed in My Leadership Approach

After the thesis, I started leading differently:

- I **started asking my team how they preferred to be led**.
- I paid more attention to how **authority is perceived** in different cultures.
- I added **more structure when needed**, even if it felt "less empowering."
- I began viewing leadership not as a badge I wear, but as a **behavior I adjust.**

Because leadership isn't about being liked.
It's about **creating conditions where the team can succeed together.**

8.4. Key Takeaways & Try This in Your Life

Most people think a PhD is about intelligence.
It's not.
It's about resilience, reflection, and relentless curiosity, the kind that keeps going long after the motivation fades.

Yes, I learned how to build a research framework.
Yes, I pushed myself to the brink of burnout and back.
But the real reward?

It taught me that **leadership is never about what you know; it's about how well you adapt.**

✅ Key Takeaways

1. Leadership Is Not Universal

What works in one culture may fail in another. Servant leadership might inspire one team and confuse another. The real skill? Knowing when to shift gears.

2. Context Is the Real Project Constraint

In project management, we talk about scope, cost, and time. In leadership, the real constraint is context. Ignore it, and even your best efforts can collapse.

3. Multicultural Teams Require Multidimensional Thinking

Assume nothing. Ask more. Observe the invisible dynamics, hierarchy, silence, participation, and adjust accordingly. Don't "treat everyone the same." **Treat everyone with what they need.**

4. Emotions Matter, but So Does Clarity

Support, encouragement, and empathy are great. But when the project is on fire, sometimes your team needs a decision, not a group hug.

5. Education Is a Project Too

Your growth isn't just a personal journey. It's a long-term project. Set goals. Track progress. Reflect deeply. And **celebrate not just what you complete, but who you become.**

🛠 Try This in Your Life

🔄 Mini Exercise: Situational Leadership Self-Audit

Ask yourself the following five questions and write down honest answers:

Question	Reflection
What's my default leadership style under pressure?	
Have I ever used a leadership approach that backfired? Why?	
How do I respond to people who challenge my ideas?	
Do I adapt my communication style to match my audience?	
Have I ever asked my team what leadership style *they* prefer?	

Then ask 2-3 people from different cultural backgrounds or team roles:

"What leadership behavior helps you do your best work?"

You might be surprised and changed by what you hear.

📌 Final Thought

The most humbling lesson of my PhD journey was this:

The best leaders don't master one style.
They master the moment and choose what's needed for the team, not their ego.
When to include, and when to direct.
When to listen, and when to act.

And in a world where your next project might span time zones, belief systems, and cultural cues... that flexibility is not just nice to have.

It's what makes you **truly global.**

CHAPTER 09

Navigating the COVID-19 Era: Crisis Mode, Control Freakery, and Quiet Transformation

"In the midst of chaos, there is also opportunity."
—Sun Tzu

9.1. The World Hit Pause, My Brain Hit Play

I still remember the moment.

A press conference.
A closed airport.
A calendar full of cross-regional strategy meetings were wiped clean overnight.

One minute, I was leading the Project Management Office (PMO) for the world's largest payment provider, working across Central and Eastern Europe, the Middle East, and Africa. We were orchestrating large-scale product development, complex technical programs, and business-critical delivery initiatives.

The next?
Locked in my apartment in Dubai, trying to run a multi-billion-dollar regional PMO... from my laptop... in sweatpants.

COVID-19 didn't just disrupt projects; it became the project.
One no one scoped, budgeted, or approved in any steering committee.

🚧 From Acceleration to Stabilization

In my organization, we were already operating at a fast pace.
The CEMEA region (Central and Eastern Europe, the Middle East, and Africa) is vast, varied, and deeply complex.

But when COVID hit, even "fast" had to be redefined.

Suddenly:

- Entire markets went cashless overnight.
- Merchants were scrambling for digital solutions.
- Issuers and acquirers needed rapid platform upgrades.
- Risk teams were working overtime.
- And every product launch timeline had to be re-evaluated, reprioritized, or paused.

Meanwhile, I was managing all of it remotely with project managers spread across time zones, stakeholders in panic mode, and delivery teams adjusting to a **fully virtual operating model.**

It was like trying to build a plane midair during a thunderstorm.

🧠 The PM Mindset That Kept Me Grounded

In the chaos, my instinct was simple: structure the unstructured.

I leaned hard into my PM toolbox:

- Rebuilt **risk registers** with pandemic variables.
- Created **project tiering** frameworks to quickly prioritize initiatives.
- Shifted our steering model from quarterly to **weekly reviews** for high-risk items.

- Supported project managers in **redefining stakeholder engagement** for a virtual world.
- Initiated **wellness check-ins**, not just status meetings, because our team wasn't just managing projects, they were managing fear, family, and fatigue.

And yes, I turned part of my living room into a command center.

Because if we were going to keep critical payment products and infrastructure moving through a global crisis, we couldn't just "adapt;" we had to **evolve. Fast.**

✍ But the Bigger Shift Was Internal

With everything on pause, travel, social life, and long commutes, **my internal monologue got louder**.

What kind of leader was I becoming?
What kind of life were we really building in Dubai?
Was I serving the mission I wanted to serve, or just running from project to project?

The stillness of lockdown created space for questions I'd long ignored.
It slowed the world down just enough for me to start listening to myself again.

And somewhere between the Zoom marathons and the sanitizing frenzy, I quietly started drafting **a new roadmap**, not for my organization, but for **my own future**.

One that eventually led to:

- A country change
- A career shift
- A whole new phase of purpose

But that clarity only came because I let myself treat the crisis **like a project** with phases, retrospectives, and a very human stakeholder at the center: *myself.*

9.2. Managing the Unmanageable: Project Lessons from a Global Lockdown

In project management, we're trained to handle **known unknowns**.
Things like resource delays, scope creep, and shifting priorities.

But COVID-19?
It was a black swan wrapped in a fog of uncertainty, masked, unpredictable, and shattering everything you thought you had under control.

And yet, oddly enough, my training kicked in.

I didn't have a playbook for a pandemic.
But I had something just as powerful:

A mindset that says, *"When things fall apart, make a plan, even if it's a temporary one."*

Here's what I learned about managing the unmanageable.

🔄 1. Work in the Rolling Waves

You couldn't plan 6 months ahead.
You couldn't even plan 6 weeks ahead.

So, we adopted **rolling wave planning**, revisiting key initiatives weekly and redefining what was realistic for the short term.
The simple truth? Forecast less, adapt more.

We made it okay to revise timelines.
To kill projects that were no longer relevant.
To scale back without shame.

It wasn't weakness.
It was **responsive leadership.**

---

2. Stabilize the Team Before the Project

During those early lockdown months, I made a key shift in my leadership priorities:

- First question in team check-ins: *"How are you feeling?"*

- Second question: *"What support do you need?"*
- Third question: *"What can we realistically deliver this week?"*

Because people don't care about deliverables when they're in survival mode.

Mental health wasn't a side topic anymore; it was a project dependency.

Some people were working in isolation.
Some had kids interrupting calls.
Some were worried about family back home.

We gave people grace.
And in return, they gave what they could, sometimes their best, sometimes just enough. And that was okay.

📊 3. Build Clarity in the Fog

When external clarity disappears, **internal clarity becomes everything**.

I made sure our team had:

- **Clear weekly priorities**
- **Streamlined reporting** (no "status theater")
- **Rapid escalation channels**
- **Transparent backlog of paused or reshaped projects**

We didn't chase certainty. We built stability, week by week, sprint by sprint.

🔁 4. Run Micro-Retrospectives

With everything shifting so fast, traditional retrospectives felt outdated.

That's why we introduced **10-minute micro-retros** every Friday:

- What went well this week?
- What didn't?
- What's one thing we'll try differently next week?

No slide decks. No overthinking.
Just a simple reflection in real-time.

It became our pulse check, and sometimes our therapy session.

🧠 5. Redefine "Success" on the Fly

Before COVID, success was measured in releases, OKRs, and stakeholder reviews.

During COVID?
Some weeks, success was:

- Keeping the team healthy
- Keeping the lights on
- Shipping **anything** at all

We normalized "slowing down to speed up."
And we made space for **personal victories**, learning something new, showing up consistently, and supporting a teammate.

In a world that was unraveling, progress, however small, was a radical act of leadership.

9.3. From Survival to Redesign: How COVID Changed the Way I Lead (and Live)

Live in "crisis mode" long enough, and it changes you.

At first, COVID forced me into **survival thinking**:

- What can we deliver this week?
- What does the team need right now?
- How do I keep the machine running without breaking the people inside it?

But as the fog started to lift and the world adjusted to its new shape, a new question began to emerge:

"What's worth keeping from this experience? And what needs to change, for good?"

Because as much as the pandemic took, it also **revealed**.

A Leadership Redesign

Before COVID, I was always on.

Leading multiple programs.
Overcommitting.
Keeping a tightly wound calendar and a mental checklist that never ended.

But the pandemic slowed me down just long enough to see what was broken in that approach.

So, I redesigned my leadership around 3 core shifts:

---

1. Less Control, More Context

I stopped trying to control everything.
Instead, I focused on creating **context**, the why, the priorities, the values.

Then I trusted my colleagues to navigate the how.

Micromanaging doesn't scale in a crisis.
Empowering people does.

---

2. Less Speed, More Sustainability

Before: I was always sprinting.

After: I learned to value **cadence over chaos**.

We introduced:

- Timeboxing to prevent burnout.
- Focused weeks without meetings.
- Energy check-ins in retros.

I stopped being proud of how many hours I worked and started celebrating how smartly we worked.

---

3. Less Noise, More Meaning

I asked better questions:

- Does this initiative *actually* matter?

- Is this meeting *really* needed?
- Is this person *seen and supported*?

COVID taught me to cut the noise and zoom in on what creates **real value, human and business alike.**

🌍 A Personal Pivot

Outside of work, something else was quietly shifting.

My wife and I had been reflecting deeply on life in Dubai, the distance from family, and the kind of future we were building.

And in the final stages of the pandemic, we made a bold decision:

We would move again, this time, to the Netherlands.

For my wife, it was a career switch.
For me, it was a full-circle moment: a chance to apply everything I had learned in one of the most structured, organized countries on earth.

It was terrifying.
And liberating.

COVID tested my limits, but it also revealed my potential.
It made me more human.
More reflective.
More intentional.

9.4. Key Takeaways & Try This in Your Life

The pandemic was a forced pause.
A hard reset.
A global retrospective no one asked for, but one we all needed.

It stripped away the non-essential.
Magnified what was broken.
And gave each of us a chance to ask:

"If life is a project..., am I managing it with intention?"

Here's what I took with me from that season:

✅ Key Takeaways

1. Crisis Reveals Character, and Systems

The first few weeks of COVID didn't create chaos. They **exposed** it.
Weak communication, unclear priorities, and poor leadership all showed up fast.
In crisis, what's hidden becomes visible. And the best leaders don't hide from it. They **respond with clarity and calm.**

2. Resilience Needs Rituals

I didn't power through it.
I structured my way through it.
Morning check-ins. Time-boxed focus. Mental health space. Micro-retros.
Because resilience isn't just grit, it's **design.**

3. The Best Plans Are Flexible

The teams that thrived weren't the ones with perfect roadmaps.
They were the ones who could pivot, prioritize, and pause without panic.
Flexibility is no longer a soft skill. It's a survival skill.

4. Remote Work Needs More Than Tech

You can't just send people home and expect the same output.
You need new ways of checking in, celebrating progress, and staying emotionally connected.
Digital tools don't build culture. People do.

5. Crisis Can Be a Catalyst

COVID forced hard questions but also created space for better answers.
It sparked new ideas. Ended old habits.
And gave us permission to stop performing and start intentionally redesigning our lives.

🛠 Try This in Your Life

Build Your Personal "Crisis Management Toolkit"

Even if you're not in a global pandemic, life will always throw curveballs.
So, build a lightweight, adaptable system for staying grounded in chaos:

Tool	What It Does	Example
Weekly Retro	Keeps momentum & reflection alive	Every Friday: What worked? What didn't?
Energy Log	Helps you track & manage burnout	Log your focus levels & stress triggers for 2 weeks
Priority Matrix	Cuts through the noise	Use the Eisenhower Matrix: Urgent vs. Important
Support System Map	Keeps you connected	List three people you can vent to, ask advice from, or laugh with
Reboot Ritual	Helps reset when overwhelmed	15-minute walk, journaling, playlist, or "no-input" time

---

💡 *PM Thought to Keep in Mind:*

"In every crisis, there is always one project you can manage, your response."

CHAPTER 10

Buying a House: How We Renovated a Home (and Stayed Married Through It)

"The ache for home lives in all of us, the safe place where we can go as we are and not be questioned."
—Maya Angelou

10.1. From New Country to New Chaos

Moving to a new country is exciting.
Buying your first home there? Even more so.
Renovating that home from the ground up... in a language I do not speak at all... during a global supply chain meltdown?

Let's just say the excitement wore off by the time I met my 12th contractor.

After landing in the Netherlands for my wife's career switch, we wanted to settle in quickly.
We were dreaming of a charming, character-filled home.
You know, something with soul.

Well, we found it after searching for around 3 months.

A beautiful early 1900s house full of potential.

Which, of course, was code for:

- Crumbling insulation
- Outdated wiring
- A bathroom from another century (possibly two)
- Enough renovation work to fund a small infrastructure project.

But the bones were strong. The layout had been promised. And for some reason, we said yes.

From Dream Home to Extreme Home Makeover

The moment we got the keys, it became obvious:

We hadn't bought a house. We'd bought a full-blown transformation project, complete with scope creep, time delays, and emotional risk levels worthy of a Fortune 500 meltdown.

And of course, I couldn't *not* treat it like a project.

I opened a Notion board.
Created a renovation backlog.
Defined milestones: insulation, heating, flooring, windows, kitchen, bathrooms, painting, garden.

We had a vision. A rough budget. A timeline so optimistic, even our contractor raised an eyebrow.

And what followed was 8 months of:

- Contractor negotiations
- Permit nightmares
- Supply shortages
- Scope adjustments

- Weekly cost updates
- And several "Why did we do this again?" conversations over takeout dinners eaten on a construction site.

Dutch Standards, Dutch Speed

To be fair, **finishing a full renovation in 8 months** is almost a miracle by Dutch standards.

Anyone who's renovated in the Netherlands will tell you:

"If it's done in a year, be grateful. If it's done under budget... you're hallucinating."

The bureaucracy moves slowly.
The contractor's schedules are packed.
The expectation for perfection is high.
And if you don't speak Dutch, good luck negotiating tile options or permit explanations without a Google Translate tab permanently open.

We had to adapt fast.

I had to manage the project as if I were working with multiple vendors across time zones.

Because in many ways... I actually was.

Instead of sprint reviews, we had site walkthroughs.
Instead of product demos, we had "the kitchen guy" waving at us with a measuring tape.
And instead of scope signoffs, we had "surprise" invoices that kept showing up like uninvited guests.

10.2. Turning a House into a Project: Planning, Budgeting, and Going a Little Crazy

The moment we decided to renovate the house, I did what any project manager would do:

I opened up a blank digital page and proudly titled it:

"The Renovation Master Plan – Final v1"

(And yes, there were at least six more "final" versions after that.)

This wasn't just a new home. This was a full-scale, multi-phase project with unknown dependencies, cultural complexity, limited local knowledge, and the most important stakeholder of all: **my wife.**

Phase 1 – Defining the Vision (Without Getting Divorced)

Before the first wall could be knocked down, we needed alignment.

- What did we both want?
- What was essential vs. nice-to-have?
- Where could we compromise without passive-aggressively glaring over dinner?

So, we created a **shared vision board**, listing:

- Style inspirations (modern meets traditional)
- Must-haves (underfloor heating, insulation, a working bathroom, please)
- Nice-to-haves (a small cellar, custom lighting, cozy garden nook)

Then we prioritized based on:

- Budget impact
- Timing
- Long-term value
- Marriage survival

Phase 2 – Budgeting: The Exercise in Futility

Here's a secret you learn the hard way:

Renovation budgets are a myth. A polite suggestion. A rough sketch drawn in pencil... on melting ice.

We started with a budget that felt doable.
Then we discovered:

- Electrical systems from the stone age
- A mysterious leak that involved three floors and one grumpy plumber
- Insulation requirements that turned out to be... not optional

Every "quick fix" revealed three more problems.

We began tracking costs weekly, including materials, labor, delivery, and all other fees.
Eventually, we created a "Contingency Burn Tracker" just to watch in real-time how our buffer was being eaten alive by surprises.

Key PM lesson: **always add 20–30% contingency to your life budget. Maybe 50%, especially if you're dealing with 100-year-old Dutch masonry.**

Phase 3 – Scheduling: The Illusion of Control

Our initial plan?
6 months.

Reality?
8 months, which, in Dutch renovation time, is basically Formula 1.

Contractors were elusive.
Materials were delayed.
Suddenly, we were running a **hybrid project**:

- Some things Agile (kitchen supplier: "We'll figure it out next week.")
- Some things Waterfall (bathroom tiling: "Once it starts, it cannot stop.")

We ended up using a **Kanban board** to track:

- In Progress (aka chaos)
- Blocked (aka "waiting for the guy")
- Delivered (aka small victory dance)
- To Review (aka "Does this even work?")

Every time we moved a task card to "Done," it felt like completing a level in a video game. Except the prize was a working light switch.

Phase 4 – Scope Control (Or How I Stopped Saying Yes)

Halfway through, we made a rule:

No new ideas unless they solve a problem or prevent a divorce.

Because scope creep in home renovation isn't just about features, it's emotional.

You see a new light fixture. You suddenly want to redo the hallway.
You fix the floor, and now the walls look sad.
And before you know it, your modest update turns into a full-blown Netflix limited series, season 2 pending.

That's when we put a cap on creativity.
Decisions went through a filter:

- Is it worth the extra cost?
- Does it delay our move-in date?
- Do we both love it, or are we just tired of choosing?
- Will Future Us care about this in 6 months?

If the answer wasn't a clear yes, we said no.
And guess what? The house still turned out beautiful.

10.3. When the Dust Settles: What the Renovation Taught Me About Real-Life Project Delivery

When you manage enough projects, you start to think you've seen it all.

Then your ceiling collapses mid-tile installation, and you realize...

Real-life projects have a personality of their own:

- They don't read your risk register.
- They don't follow your Gantt chart.
- And they definitely don't care that you're trying to stick to scope.

By the time we finally walked barefoot on our brand-new floors, I realized this renovation had taught me more about **real-world project delivery** than any certification or boardroom ever had.

Here's what stuck with me:

🛠 1. You Can't Outsource Ownership

Yes, we hired contractors.
Yes, we worked with suppliers and specialists.

But at the end of the day, if something went wrong, **it was on us.**

We had to:

- Follow up.
- Ask hard questions.
- Double-check measurements.
- Decode Dutch building codes (shoutout to Google Translate)

The lesson?

Delegation ≠ abdication.
You can trust the team, but you must own the outcome.

🔁 2. Feedback Loops Matter More Than Timelines

We learned (the hard way) that one small miscommunication could delay a milestone by **weeks**.

So, we started running:

- Daily site check-ins.
- End-of-week walkthroughs.
- Visual updates (photos, floor plans, 3D renderings)
- Voice notes with instant feedback because email chains were too slow.

It became clear:

If you're not talking early and often, you're not managing risk; you're managing surprises.

📏 3. Complexity Needs Simplicity

At one point, we had:

- 1 main contractor
- Five other suppliers
- Two municipal permits
- A temporary living space 15 minutes away
- And approximately 387 WhatsApp groups, most named with random emojis.

Everything was interconnected, and chaos was lurking.

That's when I simplified:

- Centralized our plans on one digital board.
- Assigned owners for each mini-project.
- Color-coded the backlog (God bless color coding)
- Kept daily tasks to a *max of three priorities.*

Complexity will always creep in, but clarity is what keeps things moving.

---

4. Emotional Management is Project Management

There were moments, usually around 11 p.m., with dust in the air and invoices on the table, when emotions ran high.

We argued over flooring samples.
We panicked over late deliveries.
We second-guessed decisions we made three weeks earlier.

And in those moments, I learned:

Keeping the project on track meant keeping **us** on track.

A well-timed break, a takeout night, or a "we'll decide tomorrow" truce saved us more time and money than any tool or technique.

Your team is your project's heartbeat.
When the heartbeat is stressed, the whole system misfires.

10.4. Key Takeaways & Try This in Your Life

Renovating a house isn't just about walls and wiring.
It's about vision, resilience, compromise, and an endless supply of black tea.

It taught me how real-world projects are messy, emotional, and gloriously unpredictable.
It reminded me that **PM isn't just a profession, it's a life skill**. One that can hold you together when everything else feels like it's falling apart (or off the wall, literally).

✅ Key Takeaways

1. Scope Creep Lives in Your Imagination

One Pinterest scroll or showroom visit can derail your entire plan. The key is knowing when to chase beauty… and when to chase the finish line.

2. Stakeholder Management is a Daily Practice

You don't just align once. You realign constantly, especially when your top stakeholder also happens to be your spouse and co-decision-maker.

3. Buffers Are Not Optional. They're Survival.

Bake buffers into every part of your life project. You'll thank yourself when the "kitchen delay due to missing hinge brackets" hits.

4. Done is Better Than Perfect

Some things can (and should) wait for "Version 2.0." The goal is habitability, not perfection.

5. Progress Feels Better Than Plans

Plans are lovely… but progress, however slow, is the true motivator. Move one step at a time. Celebrate each one.

🛠 Try This in Your Life

🏡 Mini Exercise: Life Renovation Backlog

Treat any major life change, be it a home makeover, a career shift, or a personal goal, like a renovation. Create a **"Life Renovation Backlog"** and sort tasks like this:

Priority	Action	Notes
Must-Have	[e.g., Finish CV rewrite / Install heating]	Core to your goal
Should-Have	[e.g., Learn Dutch / Fix lighting]	Adds value, but not urgent
Could-Have	[e.g., Redecorate / Take a course]	Nice-to-do
Won't-Have (for now)	[e.g., Landscape garden / Write a memoir]	Park for later, protect your sanity

This approach keeps your energy focused, your plans grounded, and your sanity intact.

💬 *PM Thought to Remember:*

"Every house has hidden cracks. Every life project will have delays. But with the right mindset, you don't just survive. You build something beautiful."

🛠 Bonus Tool: Renovation Change Register

Use a simple table like this to track change requests and make smarter, emotionally balanced decisions during any renovation (or major life project). It helps keep scope creep, budget bloat, and miscommunication in check, especially when working with multiple stakeholders (and spouses!).

Change Description	Requested By	Impact on Budget (EUR)	Impact on Timeline (Weeks)	Status	Decision Rationale
Upgrade kitchen appliances from standard to premium	Ozgur	2500	5	Approved	Better durability and design are agreed upon as added value
Add underfloor heating to the second bathroom.	Spouse	1800	3	Approved	Comfort-oriented, adds resale value
Switch from laminate to oak wood flooring in the living room	Both	3200	4	Rejected	Too costly for aesthetic gain, excluded from the current scope
Reposition garden lights based on the new design	Spouse	400	1	Approved	Minor effort, improves ambiance, approved

CHAPTER 11

The Wellbeing Project: When the Project Is You

"Almost everything will work again if you unplug it for a few minutes… including you."
—Anne Lamott

11.1. When the Strongest One Breaks

From the outside, everything looked great.

I had a successful career.
A solid resume.
A reputation for getting things done even under pressure.
I was the one who *others* came to when things got tough.

But quietly, beneath the surface, I was unraveling.

It wasn't one dramatic event.
No explosion. No breakdown in the middle of a boardroom.
Just a slow, creeping erosion of my mental and emotional bandwidth.

And the hardest part?

I never saw it coming.

People like me don't "burn out."
We adapt.
We push harder.
We keep it all together until we can't.

The Real Trigger: A Toxic Environment Disguised as "High Performance"

The job wasn't supposed to be toxic.
On paper, it looked amazing.
A senior role. Good brand. Ambitious projects.

But behind the scenes, it was a different story.

I found myself reporting to a **classic micromanager**, the kind who:

- Questions every decision.
- Nitpicks every sentence.
- Undermines you in meetings.
- Withholds approval just to stay in control.
- Smiles in public but criticizes in private.

At first, I tried to manage up.
I adjusted my communication. I over-prepared. I tried to "win them over."

But the more I bent, the worse it got.
And slowly, I lost sight of who I was.

I second-guessed every move.
I felt anxious before every email.
I stopped sleeping.

And then came the panic attacks.

😰 The Moment I Thought I Was Going to Die

It was a random Tuesday.

Nothing dramatic had happened that day, just a regular work meeting, a long to-do list, and the usual micromanagement loop.

But that night, as I tried to sleep, something strange happened.

My heart was racing.
My chest felt tight.
I couldn't breathe properly.
And I was convinced, absolutely convinced, that I was dying.

I sat up in bed, panicked, gasping for air.

"Is this a heart attack?"
"Is something wrong with my lungs?"
"Should I go to the hospital?"

It took hours to calm down. And it wasn't the last time.

The attacks came back in waves, always unexpected, always terrifying.
And that's when I knew: **This wasn't stress.**
This was survival mode with the brakes cut.

This was **burnout.**

🧠 A Lifetime of Pressure... Cracking at Once

Looking back, I realized this wasn't just about one bad boss.
It was the result of a **lifetime of emotional weight** I'd carried without complaint.

- Growing up with loss and trauma
- Pushing through hardship without ever slowing down
- Always being the dependable one, the strong one, the achiever
- Saying yes when I should've said no
- People-pleasing my way into exhaustion

I had spent years building resilience...
But I'd forgotten to build **boundaries**.

And without those, even the strongest structure eventually collapses.

11.2. Turning Recovery into a Project

At some point, the panic attacks stopped surprising me.
They became part of the routine.

That's when it hit me:

"I'm managing million-euro portfolios with Gantt charts and risk logs, yet I have no roadmap for myself."

It was such a strange realization.
I'd been applying structured thinking to projects for years, but I had never turned those techniques inward.

So, I did the only thing I knew how to do when faced with something chaotic and overwhelming:

I treated my **recovery** like a **project**.

And you know what?
It worked.

🛠 **Project: Rebuild Me**

📌 **Objective:**

Rebuild my emotional, mental, and physical well-being, sustainably and intentionally, after prolonged burnout.

📅 **Timeline:**

Flexible, iterative. No unrealistic deadlines. But progress had to be **visible**.

🧩 **Key Phases:**

1. **Stabilization**
2. **Decompression**
3. **Self-discovery**
4. **Reconstruction**
5. **Maintenance**

Let's break those down.

🛟 Phase 1: Stabilization – Hitting Pause to Save Myself

The first step wasn't a productivity hack.
It wasn't journaling, breathing exercises, or any of the usual wellness advice you see online.

It was a simple, difficult, and necessary decision: I had to stop.

Under the guidance of my doctor, I took time off from work.
Not a long weekend.
Not "working from home with less pressure."

A full reset.

Because at that point, my system was no longer responding to adjustments.
I was beyond tired. Beyond stressed.
I was in full survival mode, and pretending I was fine was only making things worse.

I stepped away from everything to stabilize, physically, mentally, and emotionally.

I call it **"Me Time 1.0."**
Not a luxury. A lifeline. A restart button I didn't know I needed.

During that time, I didn't try to be productive.
I focused on the basics:

- Sleep on time every night
- Meals, simple and regular
- Movement, gentle and intentional
- Silence, not to fix, just to feel.

Slowly, the panic began to ease.
My breath came back.
The noise in my head softened.

And for the first time in months, I didn't feel like I was drowning.

That's when it clicked:
This wasn't a detour in my career.
This was the launch of the most important project I'd ever managed, **my own recovery.**

Phase 2: Decompression – Learning to Do Nothing (and Be Okay with It)

After the initial fog lifted, something strange happened.

With no back-to-back meetings, no team check-ins, no dashboards to update... I didn't know what to do with myself.

The stillness felt foreign.
Even uncomfortable.
But I knew I had to **sit with it** instead of rushing to fill the space.

So, I gave myself permission to **decompress**.

This wasn't a productivity sprint. It was a **nervous system recovery plan**.

I spent this phase:

- Taking long, tech-free walks
- Journaling, with no expectation to find answers
- Reading things that inspired, not instructed
- Sitting in silence, even if it made me restless
- Letting go of guilt for not "doing more"

One of the hardest realizations was this:

I had been outsourcing my worth to my output for years.
Without a task list, I wasn't sure who I was.

This phase helped me begin to remember.

Phase 3: Self-Audit: What Stays, What Goes

Once the noise had quietened, I could finally hear myself again.

And what I heard was... revealing.

I started an exercise I now call my **Personal Inventory**:

- I made a list of every responsibility, relationship, and habit in my life.
- For each, I asked: *Does this energize me or drain me?*
- I color-coded them, green (nourishing), yellow (neutral), red (exhausting)

What I found shocked me:

- Some "success habits" were actually stress loops.
- Some friendships were built on obligation, not care.
- Some parts of my job, even the impressive ones, had been silently wounding me for years.

This was my **big decluttering**, not of my closet, but of my identity.

I began to let go of:

- The Roles I didn't need to play.
- The Goals I didn't truly care about.
- The idea that I needed to prove my value constantly.

It was both terrifying and liberating.
But it cleared the space I needed for the next phase.

🧱 Phase 4: Reconstruction – Designing a Life That Doesn't Burn Me Out

With space cleared and insight gained, I began the slow, careful process of building again.

But this time, I wasn't building a career path or a five-year plan.
I was building **a sustainable version of me.**

I asked myself:

- What kind of work rhythm supports and does not deplete me?
- What do I want my *average week* to feel like?
- What boundaries are non-negotiable moving forward?

Then I made real changes:

- Structured my days around energy, not just urgency.
- Said no to tasks that didn't align, even when they were shiny.
- Blocked recovery space *in* my calendar.
- Practiced pausing before responding, especially to triggers.

Most importantly, I gave myself **permission to work differently**.

Not slower. Not lazier.
Just **more aligned**.

🔄 Phase 5: Maintenance – Gentle Monitoring, Not Self-Micromanagement

Recovery isn't a one-time fix.
Burnout doesn't disappear like a cold.

I knew I needed a way to **stay close to myself**, even when things picked up again.

That's why I created a simple system of check-ins:

- Weekly reflection questions: *How am I feeling? What's off? What do I need more of?*
- Monthly boundary audits: *What slipped? What held strong?*
- Energy tracking: *Which tasks or people give me fuel, and which quietly drain it?*

When the red flags creep back in, such as overthinking, sleepless nights and dread before meetings, I don't wait anymore.

I adjust immediately.
No shame. No delay.

Because now I know:

You don't wait until the roof caves in to do repairs.
You fix the cracks as they appear, **especially when the house is you.**

11.3. What Burnout Really Taught Me About Leadership

If you had asked me five years ago what makes a great leader, I might have said:

- Clear direction
- Strategic focus
- The ability to get things done under pressure.
- Decisiveness
- Accountability

All valid.
All valuable.

But none of them would have saved me from what I went through.

Because here's the brutal truth that burnout taught me:

You can't lead anyone sustainably while quietly falling apart yourself.

🧠 Old Ozgur vs. New Ozgur

Before the burnout, I believed:

- Hustle was noble.
- Saying yes was professional.
- Being overwhelmed was just part of the job.
- The weight I carried was proof of my strength.

After the burnout, I understood:

- **The rest is strategy.**
- **Boundaries are leadership tools.**
- **Saying no is protecting what matters.**
- **And your nervous system is a stakeholder, too.**

I didn't just need to work differently.
I needed to **lead differently**, starting with myself.

💬 From Manager of Projects to Steward of People

My definition of leadership began to shift from:

"Deliver outcomes at any cost."

to

"Deliver outcomes *with care*, so people, including me, don't become the cost."

I became more intentional with:

- How I speak to my team (and myself)

- What I model in terms of availability and boundaries
- What I reward (busyness ≠ effectiveness)
- How I respond when someone says, *"I'm not okay"*

Because I had lived it.
And I knew what silence costs.

I Stopped Worshipping Performance

One of the hardest and most liberating lessons?

High performance isn't worth it if it comes with high pain.
And perfectionism isn't professionalism; it's **fear in a business suit.**

I stopped equating my value with my output.
I started building a culture where it was safe to ask:

- "Can we rethink this?"
- "Is this deadline realistic?"
- "Can I take a pause and come back stronger?"

And surprisingly?
The results got **better.**

Less churn.
Less hidden resentment.
More honest conversations.
And a quieter mind at the end of the day.

Leading with Soft Power

Burnout taught me that **strength isn't about pushing through.**
It's about knowing *when to pause*.
When to speak up.
When to protect the space around you, so others can breathe too.

Now, I look for:

Self-awareness over charisma

Boundaries over bravado

Empathy over ego

Leaders who admit when they're tired and build teams that make space for it.

That's the leader I'm becoming.
One project at a time.

11.4. Key Takeaways & Try This in Your Life

Burnout doesn't ring the doorbell.
It creeps in quietly and systematically.
And by the time you notice, it's too late for a "long weekend" fix.

That's why this chapter matters, not just for the exhausted professionals, but for the high achievers, the silent strugglers, and the "strong ones" who've never given themselves permission to break.

✅ Key Takeaways

1. Burnout is a project that starts in silence

You won't see it in your calendar.
It doesn't show up in performance reviews.
But it's there, in the anxiety, in the dread, in the nights you can't sleep.

2. A toxic environment will drain even the healthiest person

It's not about resilience. It's about **exposure**.
If your workplace treats exhaustion as excellence, the system is sick, not you.

3. You are a stakeholder in your own life

If your life had a risk register, your name would be the critical dependency. Your physical, emotional, and mental health are *dependencies*. Treat them that way.

4. Recovery needs structure, not pressure

You don't bounce back by grinding harder.
You recover by building a new system, slowly, intentionally, and with fewer open loops.

5. Leading well starts with living well

If you want to build teams that thrive, you need to model what thriving looks like.
That means boundaries. That means honesty. That means letting go of the "always on" myth.

🛠 Try This in Your Life

⚠ Weekly Burnout Radar: A 5-Minute System Check

At the end of each week, answer these five questions honestly:

Question	Check-In
Did I sleep well for at least 4 nights this week?	✅ / ❌
Did I say "yes" when I wanted to say "no"?	✅ / ❌
Did I feel dread before a meeting or task?	✅ / ❌
Did I do anything purely for myself, not performance?	✅ / ❌
Did I feel proud of how I protected my time and energy?	✅ / ❌

Suppose three or more answers are ❌, pause. Rethink. Adjust.
Burnout isn't a blowout; it's erosion. Quiet. Relentless. Preventable.

💬 *PM Thought to Keep in Mind:*

"Your career is a program. Your life is the portfolio.
Confuse the two, and the whole system breaks."

CHAPTER 12

CTRL+ALT+LEAD: Writing My First Book

"You don't write because you want to say something, you write because you have something to say."
—F. Scott Fitzgerald

12.1. From Burnout to Book Deal

At first, writing wasn't part of the recovery plan.
It wasn't something my doctor suggested.
It wasn't listed in my self-care backlog.

It started quietly like a whisper.
A half-finished sentence.
A Google Doc named *"Leadership Notes: Someday Maybe."*

But the more I wrote, the more I started to breathe differently.

Each sentence gave shape to the feelings I hadn't yet processed.
Each story helped me reframe not just my experiences, but my **identity**.

And slowly, page by page, a thought crystallized:

"Maybe this isn't just therapy. Maybe this is a book."

CTRL+ALT+DELETE... but for Leadership

The idea behind *CTRL+ALT+LEAD* was simple, but also subversive.

In the computer world, we all know the famous keyboard shortcut:
CTRL + ALT + DELETE, the ultimate reboot.

And that's exactly what I felt leadership needed:
A full system refresh.

Not another book about KPIs and boardroom swagger.
Not another "10 Traits of Great Leaders" listicle in hardcover.

But something more... human.
More **real**.
A collection of insights, stories, and mindset shifts that reflect the reality I had lived through crisis, complexity, cultural change, and yes, burnout.

So, the title came naturally:

CTRL+ALT+LEAD – Resetting the Leadership

And just like that, my next great project was born.

When the Book Became a Lifeline

What surprised me wasn't that the writing helped, but how deeply it helped.

- When I felt anxious, writing gave me a channel.
- When I felt lost, it gave me direction.
- When I questioned my worth, it reminded me of the lessons I had earned the hard way.

And unlike other projects, this one didn't need approval.

It had no sponsor. No business case required.

It was mine.
Built from lived experience.
Fueled by truth.
And aligned with a deeper purpose than any promotion could offer.

Writing didn't just help me recover. It helped me reconnect with who I was and who I was becoming.

12.2. Structuring the Story: From Brain Dump to Blueprint

Writing a book sounds romantic... until you're drowning in 73 half-finished paragraphs, 12 disconnected topic ideas, and one smug blinking cursor whispering:

"So... what's your point?"

Like any ambitious project, the idea for *CTRL+ALT+LEAD* started out messy.
Loose thoughts. Story fragments. Sentences scribbled in my phone notes at 10 p.m.
Pages filled with quotes, analogies, and anecdotes, some profound and some painfully cringe.

But one thing saved me from drowning in my own ideas:

Project management.

Because let's be honest, I wasn't trying to write the next great novel.
I was trying to write a **book that worked**:

- For busy professionals
- For emerging leaders
- For people like me who needed practical insights *without* the fluff

The answer was obvious:
I mapped the scope.

Step 1: Define a Working Title and a North Star

Before anything else, I needed a **North Star**.

For me, that was this core belief:

"Leadership needs a reboot, less ego, more empathy; less control, more inclusion."

I wrote that on a sticky note and placed it on my screen.
Every story, quote, and case study I included had to serve that belief.

Step 2: Brain Dump Like There's No Tomorrow

I opened a blank document and let it all out.
No structure. No censorship.

- Lessons I learned the hard way.
- Cultural insights from leading in multicultural environments.
- Cringe-worthy mistakes I made as a first-time manager.
- Strategies that helped teams thrive.
- Questions that haunted me when I felt like a fraud

It was raw, unfiltered, and deeply personal.

Then... I walked away.

Came back two days later and asked:

"What's gold here? What's clutter?"

Step 3: Build a Chapter Framework (My Book WBS)

This was my favorite part because it felt like designing a product.

I asked myself:

- What journey am I taking the reader on?
- What transformation should they experience from Chapter 1 to the final page?

And then I broke it down like a **Work Breakdown Structure (WBS):**

1. Resetting Mindset
2. Leading Through Change

3. Communication in Complexity
4. Inclusion, Empathy, & Impact
5. Navigating Personal Burnout
6. Real-Life Stories That Teach
7. Tools, Frameworks, and Action Steps

Each chapter had:

- A clear theme
- A personal story
- Practical frameworks or exercises
- One big idea readers could walk away with

The book started to take shape, not as a diary, but as a **toolkit with a heartbeat.**

🛠 Step 4: Set Milestones (Not Deadlines)

Deadlines made me anxious.
So I worked in **milestones** instead, aligned with energy, not urgency.

- "First Draft of Chapter 1 by the end of the week"
- "Feedback from beta readers on Chapter 3"
- "Finish editing the tools section before vacation."

It wasn't linear.
Sometimes I wrote Chapter 4 before Chapter 2.
Sometimes I rewrote the same paragraph six times.

But it kept flowing because I didn't force the timeline.
I followed the momentum.

💬 Step 5: Get Feedback, Not Permission

When I felt stuck, I didn't hide my drafts.

I sent chapters to a few trusted people:

- My wife
- Colleagues

- Friends
- A couple of mentors
- Even a few skeptical readers on purpose (to avoid the echo chamber)

Their input was gold.

Not just for the edits, but because every time someone said,

"I felt this one, it's real."

I knew I was on the right track.

12.3. Lessons Learned from Publishing (and from Myself)

They say the hardest part of writing a book is finishing it.
That's not true.

The hardest part is deciding to share it.

Hitting "publish" feels like standing in a crowded room, handing out pages from your journal, and saying:

"Here, read this. Judge me. And maybe, if it's not too much trouble, grow from it.

But that vulnerability?
That's exactly where the magic happens.

Because once the book was out, I started hearing things like:

- *"This finally explained what I couldn't put into words."*
- *"I saw myself in your story."*
- *"Thank you for saying what so many of us feel but never share."*

And I realized...

I didn't write this book for the masses,
I wrote it from the trenches, for those still in them.

From the overworked.
The overlooked.
The leaders-in-progress.

The people who are doing their best to make sense of chaos without losing their humanity.

📚 What Publishing Taught Me About Myself

🔒 Vulnerability Builds Trust

The more honest I was, the more powerful the connection became.

I thought I needed to sound "professional."
What I needed was to be **authentic**.

Leadership isn't a highlight reel.
It's a series of lessons disguised as mistakes.
And readers, real people, connect to real stories.

⏳ Done Is Better Than Perfect

If I had waited for the book to be perfect, it would still be sitting in a folder called "Draft v18-FINAL-FINAL-FORREAL.pdf."

Eventually, I had to stop editing and start **trusting**.

Not in the book.
But in the quiet power of showing up anyway.

🎯 Your Voice Has a Place

The world didn't stop when I shared my ideas.
Nobody canceled me for not quoting enough management theories.
In fact, the exact opposite happened:

People thanked me for writing in plain English.
For being honest.
For not pretending to have all the answers.

In a world full of noise, your quiet truth may be the exact note someone's been waiting to hear.

🚀 Publishing Is Not the End, It's the Launch

I thought publishing the book would be the final milestone.

It wasn't.

It became the foundation for:

- Conversations I never imagined having.
- Invites to speak, coach, and collaborate.
- The confidence to say, *"I've lived this. Let me help."*

But above all?

It became the **clearest proof** that a painful season could be **transformed into something meaningful**.

That a story, once buried under burnout, could become someone else's breakthrough.

12.4. Key Takeaways & Try This in Your Life

You don't need to be a "writer" to write.
You don't need a publisher's permission to share your story.
And you certainly don't need a perfect manuscript to say something **real**.

All you need is the courage to start and the wisdom to know that your lived experience might be someone else's breakthrough.

✅ Key Takeaways

1. Your mess is your message

You don't have to write from a place of having it all figured out.
In fact, the more uncertain your journey, the more relatable your story becomes.

2. Structure sets you free

A blank page is intimidating. A simple outline? Empowering.
Start with one idea. One story. One insight. Then build from there.

3. Vulnerability isn't a weakness, it's resonance

People don't connect with perfection.
They connect with *you*. The real, unfiltered, growing, questioning you.

4. Books aren't born. They're built.

One section at a time. One awkward draft at a time.
It's not magic, it's iteration and momentum.

5. Publishing is a leadership act

Putting your story out there is an invitation for others to reflect on theirs.
It's not ego. It's a **service.**

🛠 Try This in Your Life

✍ 15-Minute Author Jumpstart: From Story to Structure

If there's even a whisper inside you that says, "maybe I should write a book," try this:

Prompt	Your Notes
What's a lesson you learned the hard way?	
What's a story you often tell others?	
What's something people ask your advice on often?	
What frustrates you in your field that you wish would change?	
What's a chapter title that feels exciting to write?	

Once you've filled this out, highlight one row and expand it into a single page.
That's your first draft. That's your start.

💬 *PM Thought to Keep in Mind:*

"You don't have to build the whole project in a day.
But you do have to write the first line."

CHAPTER 13

The Failure Project: What a Side Hustle Taught Me About Letting Go

"I have not failed. I've just found 10,000 ways that won't work."
—*Thomas Edison*

13.1. A Dream on Four Wheels

There's a special kind of excitement that comes from hearing a well-tuned exhaust note echoing through a quiet street.

For me, that sound was more than horsepower.
It was hope. Precision. Freedom in four-stroke form.

So, when the idea of starting a **high-end modern classic car dealership** in the Netherlands struck me, I didn't hesitate.
I had the vision. The taste. The passion.

And soon enough, I had the **cars**.

- An **Aston Martin DB9**, refined, sleek, pure elegance.
- A **BMW E46 M3**, iconic, analog, a driver's dream
- An **Audi TT RS**, modern performance, compact power

These weren't random purchases. They were curated, purposeful, poetic choices.

This was going to be a boutique brand. Something *tasteful* and niche.

I wasn't just starting a side hustle; I was building a **dream garage with a business model**.

Offer unique, high-quality modern classics to an audience that wants emotion with their engineering.
Park them right in my driveway. Start small. Build a network. Go boutique. Build trust. Then scale, if it made sense.

It felt like the perfect fit.

But Vision Isn't the Same as Viability

There were signs early on, little ones that something wasn't quite clicking.

For starters:

- The **Dutch market** was more price sensitive than I'd expected. Buyers were pragmatic. Emotional purchases were rare.
- I couldn't speak Dutch, which made **building trust** in a very local, relationship-driven niche incredibly hard.
- I had **no showroom**, just my driveway. (Charming, maybe. Scalable? Not so much.)
- I was relatively **new in town**, with no existing dealer network or go-to specialists.

And while the cars were beautiful, rare, and well-maintained, the sales process was *slow*. Interest was tepid. Conversations dragged.
I started getting the sense that my dream customers might not actually live in this market.

📉 When Passion Becomes a Liability

Still, I clung to hope, like a driver gripping the wheel in a skid.

But one by one, the warning signs became realities:

- Maintenance bills added up.
- Inquiries led nowhere.
- I was checking the cars more often than when people were viewing them.

Eventually, I made the tough call: **cut my losses**.

I sold the cars back to dealers, at a loss, of course.
Not catastrophic, but enough to sting.

That dream? That "side project"? It quietly folded before it ever made a real sale.

🏁 What Came Next

Here's the funny thing:
Even though the business flopped, my love for cars never faded.

But instead of selling them, I made a simple decision:

I'd just **enjoy** them.

Today, I drive a **2006 Porsche 911 Turbo**. No showroom. No website. Just joy.
A car that makes every drive feel like a reward, not a revenue stream.

The hustle stalled.
But the passion? Still in drive.

And I learned something essential:

Sometimes, your passion isn't a product.
It's a **personal journey**, and that's more than enough.

13.2 – Scope Creep, Sunk Costs, and Silent Panic

When you start a side hustle, the dream feels simple:

Build something cool. Make some money. Maybe turn it into your next big thing.

But just like in any poorly scoped project, it's what you *don't plan for* that starts to eat you alive.

At first, this dealership idea was lean, focused, and exciting.
Buy a few beautiful cars. Photograph them. Market smartly. Sell it to the right buyer.

I even told myself:

"This isn't a business yet. Just a trial run. Let's see what happens."

But soon...

- I was importing spare parts.
- Negotiating delivery logistics
- Watching Euro-to-USD fluctuations
- Learning Dutch Road tax regulations at 11:30 PM
- Debating whether I needed insurance coverage levels written for *actual dealerships.*

And still, I hadn't made a sale.

📉 The Hidden Costs of Going All In

The biggest costs weren't financial.
(Though let's be clear, the *financial* ones hurt.)

It was the **mental drain**:

- The constant checking of classifieds.
- The delayed messages that led nowhere.
- The polite buyers who ghosted.
- Rain-soaked driveway viewings that made me question every decision.

I kept telling myself,

"It just needs a little more time..."
"Maybe one more car in the mix will attract more buyers..."
"Once I get my first sale, it'll all start rolling."

But deep down, I knew.

I was **past the point of rational assessment.**

I had fallen into the classic PM trap:
The Sunk Cost Fallacy.

🧠 PM Terms, Real-Life Spiral

- **Scope Creep?**
  Yep. I was suddenly considering a website, Dutch language marketing, and maybe even renting a garage.

- **Poor Stakeholder Alignment?**
  Absolutely. My wife was supportive, but even she started raising eyebrows at driveway logistics and mysterious maintenance bills.

- **Lack of Exit Criteria?**
  100%. I never defined a point where I'd say, "This is enough. Let's stop."

And you know what happens when you don't set a clear off-ramp?

You stay on the highway... long after the fuel light's blinking.

😶 Silent Panic

Here's the part people rarely talk about
The shame.

Not dramatic, public embarrassment.
Just a quiet, sinking feeling in your gut:

- That maybe you misjudged your capability.
- That maybe you're not the entrepreneurial type after all.
- That maybe... you're not as good at "following your passion" as Instagram makes it sound.

I didn't post about the losses.
No dramatic "I'm out" video.
Just a quiet undoing of a dream.

Letting go of the idea.
The pressure.
The dream... that wasn't working.

13.3 – The Real ROI: Lessons from the Loss

I lost money. I lost time. I carried more stress than I care to admit.
And yet, I still walked away richer.

Not financially, clearly.
But in ways I didn't expect.

Because when something you love doesn't work, it doesn't mean you failed.
It means you just got *real clarity* on what matters.

And that clarity?
That's a gift most people miss because they never risk enough to earn it.

So, here's what I gained.

💡 1. Passion is Not a Business Model

Loving something is not the same as monetizing it.

- You can adore cars and hate dealership logistics.
- You can be a brilliant strategist and still not enjoy cold calling or price negotiation.
- You can build a side hustle… and decide it's not the *right hustle for you.*

This experience taught me to **separate what I love from what I want to manage.**

I still love driving, researching, and talking about cars.
I just don't want to turn it into inventory, invoicing, and insurance quotes.

And I've made peace with that.

🔄 2. Exit Criteria Aren't Just for Projects

In professional project management, we always define success metrics.
Milestones. Exit points. Conditions for closure.

But in our personal projects?
We let emotion inflate the scope, and pride override the exit plan.

I should've defined an **exit point** before the first purchase:

"If I don't sell a car within X months..."
"If I spend more than X without a return..."
"If it begins to impact my energy or stress..."

Next time, and yes, there will be a next time for big ideas, I'll define my exit like I define my goals.

🧘 3. Letting Go Can Be a Leadership Skill

The hardest part wasn't stopping.
It was **forgiving myself**.

Letting go of:

- The sunk costs.
- The fantasy of what could've been.
- The ego hit of "maybe I'm not built for this."

But I realized:
Real leadership isn't about forcing something to work.
It's about recognizing when it doesn't and choosing to pivot with grace.

I didn't fail.
I completed a project that no longer aligned with my purpose, and that's a different kind of success.

And that's something every leader, entrepreneur, and human needs to learn.

13.4 – Key Takeaways & Try This in Your Life

You don't have to succeed at something for it to be worth doing.
Sometimes, the project that fails is the one that frees you.

That little car dealership dream?
It didn't make money.
But it taught me lessons that no classroom ever could.

✅ Key Takeaways

1. Not every passion should become a business

Sometimes it's enough to love something. Drive it. Admire it.

Turning joy into obligation can kill the spark faster than any spreadsheet.

2. If it's draining your energy, it's costing more than you think

Forget the P&L. What about your time, stress, sleep, and relationships? Mental bandwidth is your most limited and valuable resource.

3. Set your exit before you enter

Before you dive into any new venture, ask:

"What would make me pause, pivot, or pull the plug with confidence?"

4. Letting go isn't quitting. It's maturing.

Finishing a project (even one that doesn't "win") is leadership in disguise. It means you made the call and owned the outcome.

5. Your identity is not your outcome

The business didn't work.
You are *not* the business.
Detach your self-worth from your success metrics, and you'll grow faster, freer, and more authentically.

🛠 Try This in Your Life

🚧 Mini Project Risk Canvas – Before You Start Your Side Hustle

Use this simple canvas before launching any personal project or side business:

Area	Ask Yourself
Purpose	Why am I really doing this? (Passion, income, validation, boredom?)
Investment	How much time, money, and energy am I willing to invest without return?
Boundaries	What will I *not* sacrifice for this (family time, health, peace)?
Exit Criteria	What conditions would make me stop or pivot confidently?
Success Definition	What does *success* actually look like for me in this case?

Take 10 minutes. Fill it out. Revisit it monthly.
It might just save you from driving off a cliff in style.

PM Thought to Keep in Mind:

"Some projects aren't meant to scale.
They're meant to grow you. And that's worth more than any launch."

Bonus Content: Reflect on Your Own "Failure Project."

Not every project needs to succeed to be valuable. Use this journal to process your experience and turn loss into learning.

Reflection Prompt	Your Reflections
Describe the project or idea you pursued.	
What excited you most about starting it?	
At what point did you feel something wasn't working?	
What factors made it difficult to let go?	
What assumptions turned out to be wrong?	
What did you learn about yourself in the process?	
What skills, habits, or insights did you gain from this experience?	
If you could do it again, what would you change?	
What would you do exactly the same?	
How will this experience shape your next project or decision?	

CHAPTER 14

Designing My 10-Year Career Map: From Strategy to Calling

"The best way to predict the future is to create it."
—*Peter Drucker*

14.1 – Not a Midlife Shift, a Legacy Move

In my early 40s, I'm obviously not thinking about retirement.
I'm thinking about **relevance.**
About **impact.**
About how to take everything I've learned and turn it into something that lasts *beyond* the next project delivery.

The more experience I gain, the louder one idea becomes:

"Now it's time to give back."

Not because I've seen it all (far from it).
But because I've seen enough to know that the **next generation of professionals**, especially in tech and project management, need more than a framework and certifications.

They need:

- Mentorship grounded in reality.
- Lessons drawn from real life.
- Guidance that's human, not just hypothetical.

And that's where I see my next big role.
Not as a program director or transformation lead.
But as a **professor**.
A **coach.**
A sharer of stories that actually happened, in rooms where budgets were real and pressure was relentless.

💡 This Isn't Slowing Down, It's Leveling Up

This isn't about slowing down.
It's about **zooming out**.

About shifting from execution to education.
From chasing deliverables to cultivating minds.

Within the next 10 years, I want to fully transition into academia, not for prestige or credentials, but for **purpose**.

Because giving back isn't a hobby.
For me, it's a calling. A responsibility. A deeply personal kind of *project.*

🧭 And Yes, I'm Managing It Like a Long-Term Strategic Program

I've delivered multimillion-euro programs.
Led global teams.
Redesigned processes at scale.

So why wouldn't I apply the same structured thinking to my **own life transformation?**

This is a 10-year career map, not a casual "maybe someday" dream.

It has phases. Milestones. Risks. Stakeholders. Contingencies.
It's not a backup plan.
It's the *next step* of a meaningful path.

And it starts now with bold intention.

14.2 – Planning a 10-Year Journey Like a Project Manager

Some people make vision boards.
Others journal their dreams or leave them to fate.
Me? I built a **project plan**.

When it comes to something meaningful like shaping your next decade, your identity, or your legacy, you don't leave it to chance.
You treat it like a program. A beautiful, long-game transformation initiative called:

"Professor Dr. Ozgur – Version 2.0"

Here's how I've started managing this shift with the same principles I apply to my most critical corporate projects.

Phase 1 – Define the Future State

Before writing a single objective, I asked myself:

- *What kind of educator do I want to be?*
- *What kind of students do I want to serve?*
- *What values do I want to instill?*
- *What does success look like, not just for me, but for the people I teach?*

I visualized:

- A university or business school classroom where I'm not just teaching theory but sharing lived case studies.
- Writing and researching real-world topics on leadership, project management, and inclusive project environments.
- Helping students transition from unsure to unstoppable, just by showing up, fully and authentically.

That's my North Star, and every phase of this journey is oriented to it.

🔍 Phase 2 – Audit the Now

Project Managers don't just look at where they're going; they assess where they **are**.

So, I took inventory of my current assets:

✅ **Professional experience**: 20+ years across digital transformation, project delivery, and PMO leadership
✅ **Academic foundation**: Bachelor's in Electronics & Communication, Master's in Computer Engineering, MBA, and a PhD in Leadership
✅ **Current role** (which supports this transition beautifully):

- Defining and implementing PM best practices.
- Coaching and mentoring across the IT organization.
- Providing training and workshops.
- Supporting complex and strategic programs.

I'm not starting from zero.
I'm already teaching, just not in a classroom (yet).

🛠 Phase 3 – Break It Down Like a Program

Here's what my **10-Year Career Map** looks like in simplified form:

Timeframe	Focus Area	Key Milestones
Year 1–2	**Preparation**	Research academic systems, speak to professors, and publish thought leadership on PM and leadership.
Year 3–5	**Positioning**	Apply as a guest lecturer, publish academic articles, contribute to conferences, and build connections in academia.
Year 6–8	**Transition**	Begin part-time teaching or academic consulting roles while still in corporate; build course content.
Year 9–10	**Full Immersion**	Transition into a full-time academic position, potentially pursue a post-doc if needed.

Each phase includes:

- Stakeholder conversations (mentors, academic institutions, family)
- Skills gap analysis (e.g., academic publishing, formal pedagogy)
- Personal reflection checkpoints to ensure purpose drives the process.

Risk Register

Risk	Mitigation
Academic culture shock	Attend events early and build mentorship relationships.
Time constraints	Timeboxing for academic pursuits limits new commitments.
Imposter syndrome	Reframe: I bring real-world expertise academia *needs*
Financial impact	Prepare financially with a phased transition, passive income

---

14.3 – Why This Plan Matters More Than Ever

This isn't just a career goal.
It's a calling. A legacy move, not a career ladder step.

Because after more than two decades of leading projects, building teams, and navigating every kind of transformation imaginable, I've realized something:

The greatest impact I've ever had... wasn't delivering the project.
It was developing the people who delivered it with me, and watching them grow long after the project ended.

The mentee who found their voice.
The junior PM who finally understood the "why" behind the methodology.
The colleague who said, *"No one ever explained it to me like that before."*

Those moments? They last longer than any go live.

And now, I want more of those moments.
Deliberately. Systematically. At scale.

Why Academia?

Because academia offers different kinds of leadership opportunities.

- It's not about KPIs, it's about cultivating curiosity.
- It's not about deliverables, it's about direction.
- It's not about running faster; it's about helping people *start well.*

And frankly, the academic world needs more voices from **the real world**.

From people who:

- Know what it's like to fail and come back stronger.
- Can translate theory into action.
- Understand how leadership evolves in multicultural, modern, and messy environments.
- Have lived the burnout, led through the chaos, and learned the deeply human side of execution.

That's the perspective I bring.
And that's the gift I want to give.

Why Now?

Because if not now... when?

I've reached a stage in my life where I'm no longer chasing titles.
I'm chasing **meaning.**

- I want to shape the next generation of thinkers and doers.
- I want to turn my lessons, which are earned through late nights, broken plans, and brilliant recoveries, into fuel for someone else's journey.
- I want to leave behind more than decks and dashboards.

I want to leave behind **people who think better, lead better, and live better** because I helped light the path.

That's not ego.
That's the purpose.

And no deadline has ever felt more meaningful or more urgent than this one.

14.4 – Key Takeaways & Try This in Your Life

Not every project is about scaling up.
Some are about **going deeper**.

And this one, this 10-year plan, isn't about chasing more.
It's about **becoming more**.

More useful.
More intentional.
More aligned with the kind of legacy I want to live, not just leave.

✅ Key Takeaways

1. You don't have to wait for a crisis to redesign your life

Start from purpose, not panic.
The best transformations happen when you're grounded, not when you're desperate.

2. Long-term goals need short-term structure

A vision without structure is a fantasy.
Break it into phases, milestones, and reflection points just like a program roadmap.

3. Your current role might already be your launchpad

You don't always need to change companies to change direction.
Sometimes, your next chapter is already being written; **you just need to zoom out**.

4. Passion without planning is just hope. Planning without passion is just homework.

You need both the heart **and** the system.
That's how dreams become deliverables.

5. Legacy doesn't happen by accident

If you want to teach, give back, or inspire, make it part of your *plan*, not just your personality.

🛠 Try This in Your Life

📘 Mini Career Map Builder – Design Your Next 10 Years

Take 20 minutes. Fill this out honestly. Don't overthink, just respond.

Prompt	Your Reflection
Ten years from now, what will I be proud of that I dared to pursue?	
What does "impact" mean to me, and how do I want to create it?	
What career move would feel like a *contribution*, not just a promotion?	
Who do I want to be teaching, mentoring, or guiding in 10 years?	
What small step can I take this month to start building that path?	

💬 *PM Thought to Keep in Mind:*

"Vision gives you the why. Planning gives you the how.
Discipline delivers the when. Your job is to show up and trust the process."

CONCLUSION

You Are the Project That Matters Most

"The most important project you'll ever manage is the one called *you.* And when managed with intention, even your detours become meaningful deliverables."

—*Dr. Ozgur Ertem*

You've just read stories about loss, recovery, career change, burnout, love, reinvention, passion and yes, failure.

You've seen how I applied project management techniques not just to timelines and budgets, but to heartbreak, panic attacks, relocation, and a PhD.

But this book was never just about me.
It was about *you*.
Your life. Your chapters. Your missteps, pivots, and uncelebrated wins.

💡 We're All Managing Something

Even if you've never opened a Gantt chart in your life...
Even if you hate the word "project" ...
You're still managing something.

- A career you're unsure of
- A relationship that needs attention
- A body that's asking you to slow down.
- A dream that won't stay quiet.
- A story that still needs to be told.

And the truth is: **You've been managing it all along.**
Now, I just want to help you do it more **intentionally**.

🛠 What Project Management *Really* Means

It's not about status reports and deadlines.
It's not about being "organized" or "corporate."

It's about:

- Clarifying what matters.
- Communicating with care.
- Managing your energy like a limited resource.
- Building systems that support your growth, not sabotage it.
- Knowing when to pivot.
- And knowing when to pause.

That's project management.
That's life management.

✨ Your Story Is Still in Draft Mode

Maybe you're at a turning point.
Maybe you're recovering from your own burnout.
Maybe you're thriving and wondering, *"What's next?"*

Wherever you are...

You are *not* behind.
You are right on time.

You don't need to reinvent your life overnight.
You just need to treat your next step like it matters, because it does. Every project starts there.

What I Hope You Remember

- That your detours taught you more than your destinations ever could
- That letting go of one project doesn't mean you're giving up; it means you're making room.
- That you don't need to prove anything to be worthy of peace.
- That structure and soul are not enemies; they're teammates.
- That leadership starts with how you lead **yourself.**

One Final Call to Action

Grab a notebook. Or open a blank page. And answer this:

"If I were the most important project in my life..., what would I start doing differently tomorrow?"

That's it.
No pressure. No 5-year plan.

Just the *first action* on the *most meaningful roadmap* you'll ever create.

Thanks for joining me on this journey.
Thank you for letting me tell my stories and maybe stir up a few of yours.

Now go out there.
Lead.
Heal.
Build.
And never forget this:

You are the project that matters most.
With respect and belief in you always,

Ozgur

Bonus Content: 10 Books That Shifted My Thinking (and Might Shift Yours Too)

One thing I've learned?
The right book often arrives exactly when you need it and quietly changes everything.

It doesn't scream.
It won't fix everything overnight.
But it opens a door, and sometimes, that's enough.
It gives language to what you've been feeling.
Or it simply reminds you, *"You're not crazy. You're just growing."*

Throughout the twists and turns I've shared in this book, from burnout to breakthroughs, career transitions to personal healing, these ten books have served as anchors, catalysts, and silent mentors.

I'm sharing them with you not as a must-read checklist, but as **invitations**. To reflect. To rethink. And maybe... to relaunch something within you.

---

10 The Books That Left a Mark

1. Mind Over Mood by Dennis Greenberger & Christine A. Padesky

It is not just a book; this is therapy on paper. Helped me rewire my thoughts when anxiety was writing its own narrative.

2. The Culture Map by Erin Meyer

If you've ever worked across borders (or just want to understand people better), this is your new decoding tool.

3. The Other Side of the Couch by Gary Small & Gigi Vorgan

Fascinating, sometimes chilling, and strangely comforting. A peek into the minds that help others find clarity.

4. Man's Search for Meaning by Viktor E. Frankl

A book I revisit when I need to remember what really matters. Heavy, yes, but powerfully human.

5. The 7 Habits of Highly Effective People by Stephen R. Covey

Timeless. Practical. And way more than productivity. This is a blueprint for intentional living.

6. Daring Greatly by Brené Brown

For anyone who's ever thought vulnerability was weakness (hi, former me), this one will lovingly wreck your ego.

7. Atomic Habits by James Clear

Small hinges really swing big doors. Helped me build consistency in the middle of chaos.

8. How to Win Friends and Influence People by Dale Carnegie

Old-school charm, but still gold. Taught me that relationships are the real currency of leadership.

9. The Lean Startup by Eric Ries

Even if you're not building a business, this book teaches you how to **fail smarter and pivot faster**, which applies to just about everything.

10. Designing Your Life by Bill Burnett & Dave Evans

When I was rethinking what my future could look like, this book showed me how to prototype a life, not just plan it.

📌 *Final thought?*
Books won't fix everything.
But the right one, at the right moment, can light a path through doubt, fear, or stagnation.

May one of these light something in you.
And may your own story, messy, beautiful, and incomplete as it may feel, keep turning its pages with purpose.

About the Author

Dr. Ozgur Ertem is not your typical project leader. With over twenty years of experience spanning global IT programs, leadership development, and cross-cultural mentoring, he's known for one thing above all: turning life's messiest moments into structured, meaningful progress.

But his real credentials were earned outside the boardroom.

From losing both parents at a young age to navigating burnout later in life, Ozgur has lived the kind of personal transformation most only read about. Each setback became a project. Each challenge was a case study. Through it all, he discovered that the tools we use to manage work, planning, risk mitigation, and retrospectives can also help us manage life.

He holds a PhD in Leadership, an MBA, and multiple technical degrees, and currently leads best practice and mentoring programs at one of the world's largest IT organizations. A passionate educator at heart, Ozgur is now charting a path toward academia to help shape future generations of leaders who lead with clarity and compassion.

From Chaos to Control is his second book, following the widely praised *CTRL+ALT+LEAD: Resetting the Leadership*.

He lives in the Netherlands with his wife, their cat Gofret, and a black cherry Porsche 911 Turbo, his childhood dreams on four wheels, now lovingly restored with the same care he gives to every project, every story, and every human being he mentors.

Made in the USA
Las Vegas, NV
10 November 2026

57843568R00117